1 MONTH OF
FREE
READING

at
www.ForgottenBooks.com

By purchasing this book you are eligible for one month membership to ForgottenBooks.com, giving you unlimited access to our entire collection of over 1,000,000 titles via our web site and mobile apps.

To claim your free month visit:
www.forgottenbooks.com/free949425

ISBN 978-0-260-45667-0
PIBN 10949425

ATALOGUE OF MEMBERS

(1853–1898)

YALE CHAPTER

HI BETA KAPPA

1898

CATALOGUE OF MEMBERS

(1853–1898)

YALE CHAPTER

PHI BETA KAPPA

WITH

HISTORY AND OFFICERS

Φιλοσοφία Βίου Κυβερνήτης

1898

PRESS OF TUTTLE, MOREHOUSE & TAYLOR

PREFACE

This catalogue of members of the Yale Chapter of Phi Beta Kappa (1853–1898) is based on a list carefully prepared by the late Professor H. A. Newton, Graduate President of the Society.

The few important facts in the life of each member have been gathered from the class records deposited in the University library, to which Mr. Van Name has kindly given us access. The incompleteness of some of these records, both of entire classes and of individuals, has made adequate treatment of such cases impossible, but for all other shortcomings of the catalogue the Committee alone is responsible.

The last catalogue (1780–1852) contains the names of 1640 members: the present one 1300 members—a total of 2940 in the 118 years of the Chapter's existence; of this number about 1240 are now living.

The Committee have found the work extremely interesting and only regret that the short time allowed for its completion prevented them from re-editing the years 1780 to 1852 and incorporating these with the present issue. It is expected that the complete catalogue will be published in 1901, and in order that it may be as accurate as possible, it is urged that notification of errors in the present catalogue and notices of deaths, changes of residence, etc., be sent to the "Catalogue Committee," Phi Beta Kappa, Box 1496, New Haven, Conn.

We are deeply indebted to Mr. Franklin B. Dexter, Assistant Librarian of the University, for advice and assistance, and to Mr. George Dwight Kellogg, who has written the history of the local Chapter.

———

Phi Beta Kappa is now a firmly established institution at Yale. It has graduate and undergraduate officers, sends delegates to the meetings of the United Chapters, secures distin-

guished men to speak before the University, and holds bi-
weekly meetings of the undergraduates during their Senior
year. These have been held in the rooms of various members,
with an attendance varying from 25 to 45 men.   After
the business of the evening is disposed of, a paper is read
or talk given by one of the members, generally on some book,
with readings, followed by a general discussion.   Hereafter
the Juniors who are admitted to membership at the annual
banquet in the spring, will meet with the Seniors for the re-
mainder of the college year.

The Chapter at Yale rests entirely on a scholarship basis, the
only qualification of membership being the attainment of a
certain rank in the appointments, announced by the Faculty
at the beginning of Junior and end of Senior year.   As was decided a year ago, beginning with the class of 1900 the appoint-
ment required will be that of Philosophical Oration.   This
will raise the standard of the Society and enhance the honor
of membership.   At the same time, the large number of students in each class, the steady improvement from year to year
in preparatory and college work and the added attractions
the Society now offers, insure a sufficient membership to
make a strong, active organization.

While everything is being done to strengthen the undergraduate part of the Society and although it will continue to
be the active, legislative body, it has seemed very desirable
that the large number of graduate members should keep up
their interest in the Society and have some influence in its do-
ings.   The catalogue is only the first of the steps taken to
secure this result. A Graduate Committee has been appointed
to raise money for and have control of a Graduate Fund.   An
amendment is now before the Society, with every probability
of its being passed, requiring that this same committee shall
be consulted with regard to any change in the constitution,
and shall act as an advisory board generally.

This committee, furthermore, is to have control of the new
quarters of the Society, assigned to it by the University, rent
free, which are now being fitted up in White Hall.   The
room will be primarily for the meetings of the Society, but
undergraduates will be supplied with keys and graduates may
make use of its privileges at any time on application.   The
entire cost of fitting out the room is borne by a graduate
member, who wishes his name withheld.

In 1901, during Yale's 200th anniversary celebration, a re-union of Phi Beta Kappa men will be held and everything will be done to make it an enthusiastic gathering. The question of a society house will come up at that time, and if it is answered in the affirmative—as there is every reason and need that it should be—it is expected that several large subscriptions will be immediately pledged. The year 1901 will be also the 125th anniversary of the founding of the society.

It is not only at Yale that the possibilities of Phi Beta Kappa are being realized. Among the 39 other Chapters there are fresh signs of activity, and 15 new colleges will apply for charters at the meeting of the United Chapters to be held at Saratoga, September 7, 1898.

A Phi Beta Kappa Alumni Association was formed a few years ago in New York City, and now has a membership of several hundred graduates of the various colleges. Its gatherings are said to be most successful in the character of the addresses delivered and in the subsequent discussion. This example might well be followed elsewhere.

In these ways is the Society realizing the ends set forth in its early charters ; an "institution founded on literary principles," to promote "friendship and union" among its members.

JAMES ROBINSON SMITH ⎫ *Catalogue*
CHARLES WELLES GROSS ⎬ *Committee.*
PETER HAGNER HOLME ⎭

NEW HAVEN, May 1898.

HISTORICAL SKETCH OF PHI BETA KAPPA

Over a quarter of a century has passed since Mr. Bagg pronounced what he doubtless intended for the funeral eulogy over the Yale chapter of Phi Beta Kappa.[1] As the commencements continued to come and go without the usual oration and poem, it became clear to all, that after nearly a hundred years of honored activity, the society had fallen asleep.

But there must have been cherished at Yale, as there had been in 1781, at the College of William and Mary, when dissolution threatened that patriotic institution, "a sure and certain hope, that the Fraternity would one day rise to Life everlasting and Glory immortal."[2] That the Yale chapter at present supplies a real need, is amply evidenced by the genuine and ever increasing interest displayed by the members since the revival of initiations fourteen years ago.

The story of the inception of the Virginia chapter has been often told. Dr. Edward Everett Hale's account in the Atlantic Monthly (July, 1879), entitled "A Fossil from the Tertiary," is a peculiarly genial and sympathetic treatment. The fullest history of the Yale society down to 1871 is in Mr. Bagg's "Four Years at Yale;" while in the sixth chapter of "Harvard College by an Oxonian" (1894), Mr. George Birbeck Hill presents an Englishman's impressions of what he naively terms our "aristocracy in a democratic country." The publication in the William and Mary College Quarterly Historical Magazine (April, 1896) of the early minutes of the parent society, together with many facts of biographical, historical and antiquarian interest, has at last made accessible abundant material for the examination of this subject. Lastly should be mentioned the publications of the secretary of the United Chapters, Rev. E. B. Parsons, D.D., of Williamstown, Mass., particularly that of 1897, which gives the officers, constitution and minutes of the United Chapters, and the present officers, customs and statistics of the forty separate branches.

[1] Bagg: "Four Years at Yale," pp. 224–235.
[2] Closing words of the original record of the William and Mary parent society, published *in extenso* in the William and Mary College Quarterly, April, 1896.

The society is probably indigenous to America. All attempts to connect its origin with the spread of the order of Illuminati in Bavaria, or to make it an importation by Thomas Jefferson, have proved futile. Jefferson was, it is true, in Williamsburg on the night of December 5, 1776, when the first meeting was held in the old Raleigh Tavern, with its mansard roof and rows of dormer-windows, in the room known as the Apollo Hall, which shortly before had echoed to the ringing words of Patrick Henry ; but there is no evidence that Jefferson was in any way concerned with the organization of the society. Quite the contrary, for we may trust the Hon. William Short, president of the parent chapter from 1778 to 1781, when he writes in 1831 : " The society was formed by a student who prided himself on being the best Hellenist there, to rivalize another society with Latin initials."

The introduction of Phi Beta Kappa into New England is one of the romantic incidents of American college history. In 1779 Mr. Elisha Parmele,[1] who had resided two years in New Haven as an undergraduate, and subsequently received his bachelor's degree from Harvard in 1778, was compelled to travel south for his health. Being an earnest scholar he was no doubt attached to the flourishing college at Williamsburg,

---

[1] Rev. Elisha Parmele (in the minutes of the society he is sometimes called Elijah) afterwards settled in Lee, Mass., July 3, 1783. In 1784 the church granted him leave of absence to regain his health ; but he died suddenly, while traveling in Virginia, at the county-seat of Col. Abraham Byrd, Aug. 2, 1784, æt. 29. He has been characterized as '' sound in the faith, amiable in. disposition, distinguished for his talents, and acquirements, and eminent for his piety." (W. M. C. H. M., p. 251.)

Dr. E. E. Hale has in his possession a packet of papers and documents pertaining to Parmele, some being of especial interest, as they indicate in the young minister a high degree of scholastic attainment. Among them are to be found : a recommendation by Rev. Stephen West (Yale 1755), subscribed by Ezra Stiles, president of Yale College (1778–1795), certifying to the character of Rev. Elisha Parmele ; his last will and testament, couched in very devout language ; a manuscript Syriac grammar, bearing the date March 24, 1778, Cambridge ; a Syriac translation of Paul's Address to the Athenians ; and a Chaldee grammar ; all these last mentioned works display remarkable care in execution.

No portrait of Parmele is known to exist. The pictures once belonging to the Byrds of Westover are now the property of the Harrisons of Brandon, but Mr. Charles Washington Coleman of Williamsburg, Va., who is well acquainted with the collection, informs me that he has not been able to discover in it any likeness of young Parmele.

where according to tradition[1] he attended the lectures of Prof. George Wythe, who held the first chair of law founded in an American college.[2] There appears to be no evidence that Parmele was a tutor at that institution.

We are made certain, however, by the society's minutes, that on July 3, 1779, Parmele was initiated into the Phi Beta Kappa. To judge by the attestations of love and affection which recur in the early cipher correspondence between Virginia and Connecticut, he was highly esteemed. When he started on his northward journey, he was entrusted with two "charter parties" drawn up on Dec. 4, 1779, and with power to establish two "scyons," in Cambridge and New Haven respectively; but inasmuch as he reached New Haven first, the Yale chapter, founded Nov. 13, 1780, antedates that at Harvard, which was organized Sept. 5, 1781.

Those early days were full of trial and uncertainty, but we may learn from their rhetoric that their hopes were none the less buoyant. A letter of 1782 to the Yale chapter says: "The present revolution in America is not inferior to the events which produced a Homer, a Vergil and a Milton. What state will have the honor of giving the world a poet, who shall do justice to the establishment of American Independence?" And again from the same year: "In the event of a return to peace, I trust to see the extended influence of the Φ. B. K. in its numerous branches at no distant period produce a union through the various climes and countries of this great continent of all lovers of literary merit, founded on the broad basis of personal emulation."

The Cambridge chapter when only a yearling writes through the secretary: "I conceive that the institution of the Φ. B. K. will have a happy tendency to destroy prejudices that too frequently subsist between different Universities, and make them act on a more liberal principle, and seek the mutual advantage of the several societies with which they may by their institution be connected."

Political questions formed the staple for discussion and debate. Many of the early members became suspiciously active in politics so that some good persons shook their heads, believing that the society had been intended as a political

---

[1] Letter from Mr. Coleman, Dec. 20, 1895.
[2] W. M. C. H. M., p. 264, gives a valuable note on this "first chair of law and police."

engine.   Moreover, Jefferson's open fondness for William
Short and others of the brethren may have helped give currency to the report that he had been the original promoter of
the organization.

As a secret society "founded on literary and philosophical
principles," the Yale chapter saw its palmiest days in the first
half-century of its existence.   Not more than a third of the
Senior class could belong, the selection not being based
wholly on scholarship as in later years.   There were elaborate
initiatory formulæ ; members were brethren, and pledged
to encourage friendship, morality and science.   There was
no fixed place of meeting, although there was at times a
"usual place," which was often the "Rhetorical Chamber"
or a tutor's room.   In 1815, there were room-to-room meetings
which have been so successfully revived since 1894.   Public
meetings were often held in the old Doolittle Hall, once on
the corner of Elm and College Streets.   The annual meetings
being of especial importance and dignity, were assembled in
the old Court House on the green, whence the society often
adjourned to the Center Church if an oration was in the
order of the day.   At commencement there was a grand public
gathering of the society at which the annual poem and
oration were delivered.

We are all familiar with the solemnities of Phi Beta day at
Harvard at the present day ; a letter from the Harvard
Chapter in 1780 shows that the exercises were no less impres-
sive at that time : "We celebrated our anniversary with open
doors.   The students generally attended as well as some of
the first characters of the State, who were on business in
town.   These circumstances seemed to give dignity to the
Society, as the greatest regularity was observed by the
members.   The students paid us the highest respect standing
in their places, until we walked out in order."   Again in
1790, the Harvard chapter writes : "The Society proceeded
to the Chapel, where two orations were delivered before a
respectable and crowded audience, consisting of the governors
of the university, and other gentlemen, and a number of
ladies, and the students. . . .   After two orations the
Society retired to a house in town, where an elegant entertain-
ment was provided.   Having spent a couple of hours in con-
vivial enjoyment and drank several toasts, expressive of our
warm affection for the Society at large and our best wishes

for its interest, and having smoked the calumet of peace and philanthropy, we took an affectionate parting."

In 1831 the Harvard chapter was forced by John Quincy Adams, John Hancock, Judge Story and others in authority to abandon the oath of secrecy.[1] Yale was soon prevailed upon to follow in the movement. Mr. Charles Tracy, of the Yale class of 1832, thus graphically describes the event:[2] "In those days freemasonry and anti-masonry fought their battles ; and a grave question of conscience arose about the promise of secrecy exacted on initiation into the Phi Beta Kappa Society. Harvard was for resolving the secrecy and it sent Edward Everett to the private meeting at Yale to advocate the cause. He used a tender tone, stood half-drooping as he spoke, and touchingly set forth, that the students at Harvard had such conscientious scruples, as to keep them from taking the vow of secrecy, and the society life was thus endangered. There was stout opposition, but the motion prevailed, and the missionary returned to gladden the tender consciences of the Harvard boys. The secret of course was out. The world did not stare at the discovery ; and when a few years had passed, the society took back its secrecy and revived its grip."

By the time of the Civil War, although the annual orations and poems were continued, the private meetings had wholly lapsed, so that when the annual public literary exercises ceased in 1871, the last thread of tradition seemed to be broken. But it was not so. After a short interim a revival of the institution was proposed by the class of 1884. Several graduate members on the faculty, the late Prof. Hubert A. Newton, '50, Mr. J. Sumner Smith, '53, and Prof. Tracy Peck, '61 empowered them to reorganize the society, and initiate the class of 1885, an event which was solemnized at a modest banquet in Alumni Hall. From this time on the society flourished directly in proportion as it recognized the social possibilities which might arise from the association of a score or more of young men united by the common bond of scholastic attainment and a vigorous purpose. On March 8, 1884, as the result of a conference with Prof. Newton and others, Mr. Ambrose Tighe, '79, a tutor in the college, sug-

[1] Quincy's Harvard, II, 398 ; Hill, p. 108.
[2] Biographical sketches of the class of 1832, of Yale College, Appendix p. 22, in some reminiscences delivered before the New York Alumni Association in 1873.

gested to the society the propriety of giving a regular course of public lectures. This idea was carried out by the class of 1885. The experiment has proved successful, so that the Phi Beta Kappa course has been officially recognized in the University Catalogue. The expense of these lectures is at present met by the undergraduate members. It is hoped that before long some generous alumnus may endow a lecture fund, providing also for the publication of particularly worthy addresses.

In 1895, when the constitution of the society was redrafted, a number of important additions were made. Stated literary meetings were appointed for the first Wednesday in each month; December 5, as the anniversary meeting, was to be appropriately observed with papers and addresses of historical interest; the annual meeting and the initiation-banquet were definitely placed; and the lecture-system formally adopted. Recently the class of 1898 decided to hold their literary meetings bi-weekly, from room to room.

The banquet has always been a prominent feature. In 1813 refreshments were voted too expensive and conducive to disorder, but the custom continued with succeeding classes, although upon one occasion the college authorities interposed to stop what then seemed reckless extravagance.

There are a few facts of antiquarian interest which should be referred to briefly. The "sign" was a left to right stroking of the chin. The "grip" was an ordinary clasping of the hands without locking of thumbs, but with a slight pressure on the wrist. The "knock" consisted of three raps, two soft and one loud, in anapaestic rhythm. The college bell used to announce the time of meeting, by a rough imitation of the old society cry, "Phi ai ai, Phi Beta Kappa." The favorite refreshment for informal occasions seems to have been the humble American peanut. In the early days of secret correspondence the cipher employed was the following: u, t, m, l, z, o, y, p, v, q, d, c, r, f, h, k, n, x, b, a, i, s, g, e. The same symbol was used for *i* and *j*, and *v* and *w*.[1]

[1] The cipher alphabet can easily be determined from a letter with its translation, both to be found in the society trunk of archives deposited in the University Library. Dr. E. E. Hale writes me under date of Nov. 22, 1895 : "The Alphabet may be found in the Harvard Book, at page 344. Oddly enough, the authorities at Cambridge cannot find it in the very documents from which Mr. Dana copied the table."

The medal worn by members has varied in size at different times : at present a gold key of rather modest dimensions is preferred. Composition prizes were once awarded for the encouragement of literary activity. Proposals were once made to establish a fund for "indigent brethren," but without success. The records of the Yale chapter from 1781–1786 were lost. The three men who spirited them away in 1786 were subsequently tried and punished. Soon after the return of these priceless documents, they were again stolen, this time irrecoverably. The "trunk" deposited in the University Library contains the complete records from 1786–1846, the catalogue down to 1852, various publications of the society, manuscript essays, papers, etc., and a budget of letters from a number of distinguished men : Longfellow, Bryant, Holmes, Chancellor Kent, Calhoun, Daniel Webster, Edward Everett and Rufus Choate. The following letter from Oliver Wendell Holmes, in which he declines an honor which he was able to accept several years later, is now printed for the first time :

BOSTON, Sept. 7, 1847.
Dear Sir :

I have deferred answering your letter containing the invitation of the Φ. B. K. Society of Yale College to deliver a poem before them for the reason that I was unwilling to decline, and yet knew not how to accept.

As it is necessary, however, to decide the question without further delay, I feel myself compelled to give up the pleasure I should have had in appearing before the society of our sister college, in the view of many previous engagements of different but engrossing nature, which occupy me during many coming months. I need only say, that I could hardly make up my mind to forego this opportunity so kindly offered me, to convince you that I think my excuse is a good one.

I have never visited Yale College, where my father was educated and everything connected with which he always regarded with the deepest interest. With a hereditary right to love and venerate this noble institution, I am the one who most regrets that this kind invitation found me involved in so many engagements that it would have been unfair to have submitted myself to the judgment of such an audience as I should have had, with such preparation only as I should have found leisure to make in the midst of various distractions.

I am, with much respect,
Your obedient Servant,
O. W. HOLMES.

To Rev. E. Strong, New Haven, Conn.

It is a curious bit of literary history not generally known, that the Phi Beta Kappa poem read by Dr. Holmes in New

Haven, on Aug. 14, 1850, does not appear in his collected works under its title, "Astræa: The Balance of Illusions." In the Riverside edition, it appears among "Songs in Many Keys," broken up into several distinct poems: Spring; The Study; The Bells; Non-Resistance; The Moral Bully; The Mind's Diet; Our Limitations. The original, consisting of 39 pages, was published in 1850, by Ticknor, Reed and Fields.

For many reasons it seems a pity that the characteristic oration and poem should have been abandoned at Yale. The Harvard series contains works of the best American orators and poets, preëminently Emerson's "American Scholar" in 1837. A complete description with bibliography by Mr. William H. Tillinghast has been prepared for the Harvard Library Bulletins, 1891.

In closing let me add just a word touching the present relations of the several chapters. The clumsiness of handling society business by correspondence led in 1881 to the organization of the United Chapters, with the proper constitution and officers. A National Council consisting of the senators, and not more than three delegates from each chapter, is held triennially. The council has no power to restrict or abridge the rights or privileges now exercised by existing chapters, except as expressly provided in the constitution of that body.

The conditions in New Haven at the present day are peculiarly favorable for developing social and literary activity among the members. The centralized life of the first two years and the grouping of the best scholars into separate divisions assuring acquaintanceship; the sympathy that must arise from common ideals of scholastic attainment and seriousness of purpose; the inspiring associations that cluster about the society; these are but a few of the forces which make towards this end. The Alumni share this feeling; the Faculty have always been glad to avail themselves of the opportunity of coming into closer touch with the best scholars in each class; the undergraduate members invariably express themselves surprised to discover the depth of thought, intensity of feeling and nobleness of character that are often possessed by some of their more quiet and obscure classmates.

GEORGE DWIGHT KELLOGG.

PHI BETA KAPPA

THE UNITED CHAPTERS

OFFICERS (1895-1898)

President

Bishop HENRY C. POTTER, D.D., LL.D., New York City.

Vice-President

Hon. JOHN A. DE REMER, LL.D., Schenectady, N. Y.

Secretary and Treasurer

Rev. E. B. PARSONS, D.D., Williamstown, Mass.

SENATORS (1892-1898)

Hon. J. A. DE REMER, LL.D., (Union) Schenectady, N. Y.
Pres. M. E. GATES, LL.D., (Rochester) Amherst, Mass.
Prof. SAMUEL HART, D.D., (Trinity) Hartford, Conn.
Col. T. W. HIGGINSON, M.A., (Harvard) Cambridge, Mass.
Pres. SETH LOW, LL.D., (Columbia) New York City.
Prof. F. A. MARCH, LL.D., L.H.D., (Lafayette) Easton, Pa.
Bishop H. C. POTTER, D.D., LL.D., (Union) New York City.
Editor H. E. SCUDDER, L.H.D., (Williams) Cambridge, Mass.
Pres. F. A. WALKER, LL.D., (Amherst) Boston, Mass.
Librarian JUSTIN WINSOR, LL.D., (Harvard) Cambridge, Mass.

SENATORS (1895-1901)

Prof. S. E. BALDWIN, LL.D., (Yale) New Haven, Conn.
Prof. H. L. CHAPMAN, D.D., (Bowdoin) Brunswick, Me.
Pres. D. C. GILMAN, LL.D., (Yale) Baltimore, Md.
Rev. EDWARD E. HALE, D.D., (Harvard) Roxbury, Mass.
Bishop J. F. HURST, D.D., Washington, D.C.
Col. WILLIAM LAMB, M.A., (William and Mary) Norfolk, Va.
Prof. F. P. NASH, L.H.D., LL.D., (Hobart) Geneva, N. Y.
Rev. E. B. PARSONS, D.D., (Williams) Williamstown, Mass.
Pres. C. F. THWING, D.D., LL.D., (Harvard) Cleveland, O.
Prof. ADOLPH WERNER, PH.D., (Coll. City New York) New York City.

CHAPTERS OF PHI BETA KAPPA
(In the order fixed by the Council.)

Alpha of Maine, (Bowdoin,) Brunswick, Me.
Alpha of New Hampshire, (Dartmouth,) Hanover, N. H.
Alpha of Vermont, (State University,) Burlington, Vt.
Beta of Vermont, (Middlebury,) Middlebury, Vt.
Alpha of Massachusetts, (Harvard,) Cambridge, Mass.
Beta of Massachusetts, (Amherst,) Amherst, Mass.
Gamma of Massachusetts, (Williams,) Williamstown, Mass.
Delta of Massachusetts, (Tufts,) Tufts College, Mass.
Alpha of Connecticut, (Yale,) New Haven, Conn.
Beta of Connecticut, (Trinity,) Hartford, Conn.
Gamma of Connecticut, (Wesleyan,) Middletown, Conn.
Alpha of Rhode Island, (Brown,) Providence, R. I.
Alpha of New York, (Union,) Schenectady, N. Y.
Beta of New York, (Univ. City of New York,) New York, N. Y.
Gamma of New York, (Coll. City of New York,) New York, N. Y.
Delta of New York, (Columbia,) New York, N. Y.
Epsilon of New York, (Hamilton,) Clinton, N. Y.
Zeta of New York, (Hobart,) Geneva, N. Y.
Eta of New York, (Colgate,) Hamilton, N. Y.
Theta of New York, (Cornell,) Ithaca, N. Y.
Iota of New York, (Rochester,) Rochester, N. Y.
Alpha of New Jersey, (Rutgers,) New Brunswick, N. J.
Alpha of Pennsylvania, (Dickinson,) Carlisle, Pa.
Beta of Pennsylvania, (Lehigh,) South Bethlehem, Pa.
Gamma of Pennsylvania, (Lafayette,) Easton, Pa.
Delta of Pennsylvania, (Univ. of Penn.,) Philadelphia, Pa.
Alpha of Virginia, (William and Mary,) Williamsburg, Va.
Alpha of Ohio, (Western Reserve,) Cleveland, Ohio.
Beta of Ohio, (Kenyon,) Gambier, Ohio.
Gamma of Ohio, (Marietta,) Marietta, Ohio.
Alpha of Indiana, (De Pauw,) Greencastle, Ind.
Alpha of Illinois, (Northwestern,) Evanston, Ill.
Alpha of Kansas, (State University,) Lawrence, Kan.
Alpha of Minnesota, (State University,) Minneapolis, Minn.
Beta of Maine, (Colby,) Waterville, Me.
Kappa of New York, (Syracuse,) Syracuse, N. Y.
Epsilon of Pennsylvania, (Swarthmore,) Swarthmore, Pa.
Alpha of Maryland, (Johns Hopkins,) Baltimore, Md.
Alpha of Iowa, (State University,) Iowa City, Iowa.
Alpha of Nebraska, (State University,) Lincoln, Neb.

PRESIDENTS OF THE YALE CHAPTER

(ALPHA OF CONNECTICUT)

1853–1898

———

1853–4	ASA BACON.
1855	ROGER SHERMAN BALDWIN, LL.D.
1856	THOMAS ANTHONY THACHER, LL.D.
1857	JAMES DWIGHT DANA, LL.D.
1858–9	NOAH PORTER, D.D.
1860	JOSEPH GIBSON HOYT, LL.D.
1861	DAVID LOWREY SEYMOUR, LL.D,
1862	MILTON BADGER, D.D.
1863–5	GEORGE EDWARD DAY, D.D.
1866	ELIJAH PORTER BARROWS, D.D.
1867	HENRY BARNARD, LL.D.
1868	HORACE BINNEY, M.A.
1869–83	INCREASE NILES TARBOX, D.D.
1884–9	THEODORE DWIGHT WOOLSEY, D.D., LL.D.
1890–1	NOAH PORTER, D.D., LL.D.
1892–6	HUBERT ANSON NEWTON, LL.D.
1897–8	TRACY PECK, M.A.

GRADUATE OFFICERS OF THE YALE CHAPTER

FOR THE YEAR 1898

President

Prof. TRACY PECK, M.A.

Vice-President

Prof. ARTHUR M. WHEELER, LL.D.

Corresponding Secretary

Prof. BERNADOTTE PERRIN, LL.D.

Treasurer

J. SUMNER SMITH, M.A.

Senator

Hon. SIMEON E. BALDWIN, LL.D.

Delegates to the National Council

Prof. ARTHUR M. WHEELER, LL.D.
Prof. THOMAS D. SEYMOUR, LL.D.
Prof. BERNADOTTE PERRIN, LL.D.

———

UNDERGRADUATE OFFICERS

FROM THE CLASS OF 1898

President

SAMUEL E. BASSETT.

Vice-President

HOWARD B. WOOLSTON.

Secretary

NORMAN B. BEECHER.

Assistant Treasurer

MORTON L. FEAREY.

Executive Committee

EDWARD C. PERKINS.
GEORGE M. RIPLEY.
HENRY B. WRIGHT.

MEMBERS

The present address, so far as known, of each living member follows his name. Degrees are from Yale unless otherwise specified. m. = married. Only the main occupations and important official positions are given.

1853

WILLIAM POPE AIKEN
   M.A. b. at Fairhaven, Mass., July 9, 1825. m. Minister.
   d. 1884.

JOSHUA ANDERSON
   LL.B., M.A. b. at Buckingham, Pa., Dec. 14, 1828.
   Lawyer. d. 1864.

HENRY HARPER BABCOCK   *New Haven, Conn.*
   b. at New Haven, Conn., July 24, 1833. Business.

THEODORE BACON   *Rochester, N. Y.*
   M.A. b. at New Haven, Conn., May 6, 1834. m.
   Lawyer. Captain in Civil War.

BENJAMIN FRANKLIN BAER
   b. at Lancaster, Pa., Jan. 9, 1834. Lawyer. Captain in
   Civil War. d. 1875.

HENRY SILLIMAN BENNETT   *New York City.*
   b. at New York City, March 7, 1832. m. Lawyer.

EDWARD COKE BILLINGS
   LL.B. Harv., LL.D. b. at Hatfield, Mass., Dec. 3, 1829.
   m. Judge of U. S. District Court in La. d. 1893.

HIRAM BINGHAM   *Honolulu, H. I.*
   M.A., D.D. b. at Honolulu, H. I., Aug. 16, 1831. m.
   Missionary in Hawaiian Islands. District Secretary of
   A. B. C. F. M.

CHARLES BROOKS
   b. at Townsend, Mass., March 24, 1831. m. Minister. d.
   1866.

SAMUEL MILLS CAPRON
   M.A. b. at Uxbridge, Mass., May 15, 1832. m. Teacher.
   d. 1874.

2

EDSON LYMAN CLARK   *Hinsdale, Mass.*
  b. at Easthampton, Mass., April 1, 1827. m. Minister.
  Author of "The Arabs and the Turks," "The Races of
  European Turkey."

OLIVER ELLSWORTH COBB
  M.A. b. at New York City, March 21, 1833. m. Minister. d. 1891.

THOMAS FREDERICK DAVIES   *Detroit, Mich.*
  M.A. and Trinity, D.D. and U. of P., LL.D. Hobart. b.
  at Fairfield, Conn., Aug. 31, 1831. m. Bishop of Michigan.

JAMES METCALF GILLESPIE
  b. at Natchez, Miss., March 6, 1832. m. Cotton planter.
  d. 1892.

WILLIAM HENRY GLEASON
  M.A., D.D. Rutgers. b. at Durham, Conn., Sept. 28, 1833.
  m. Lawyer. Minister. Member of N. Y. Leg. d. 1892.

JAMES RAYMOND GOODRICH
  M.A. b. at Wethersfield, Conn., Jan. 8, 1831. Teacher.
  d. 1859.

CORNELIUS HEDGES   *Helena, Mon.*
  M.A. b. at Westfield, Mass., Oct. 28, 1831. m. Lawyer.
  Probate Judge. U. S. Attorney for Territory. Judge
  of County Court. State Senator.

ISAAC HOLT HOGAN
  b. at Glenville, N. Y., Nov. 16, 1828. Teacher. d. 1855.

GEORGE ASBURY JOHNSON
  b. at Salisbury, Md., July 27, 1829. m. Lawyer. Justice
  of Circuit Court of Indiana. Attorney General of
  California. d. 1894.

SHERMAN WILLARD KNEVALS.   *New York City.*
  b. at New Haven, Conn., Oct. 29, 1832. m. Lawyer.

CHARLTON THOMAS LEWIS   *Morristown, N. J.*
  M.A., Ph.D. U. C. N. Y. b. at Westchester, Pa., Feb. 25,
  1834. m. Letters. Professor of Greek and Math.
  Lawyer. Author of history of Germany; Latin dictionary.

JAMES M'CORMICK   *Harrisburg, Pa.*
    M.A. b. at Harrisburg, Pa., Oct. 31, 1832. m. Lawyer.

CHARLES GARDINER MCCULLY   *Calais, Me.*
    b. at New York City, Dec. 29, 1833. m. Minister.

WAYNE MACVEAGH   *Philadelphia, Pa.*
    LL.D. Amherst. b. at Ware, Mass., Oct. 11, 1832. m.
    U. S. Minister at Constantinople. U. S. Attorney General. U. S. Ambassador to Italy.

JOSEPH OLDS   *Columbus, O.*
    LL.B. Harv. b. at Circleville, O., April 15, 1832. m.
    Lawyer. Judge of Court of Common Pleas in Ohio.

BENJAMIN KINSMAN PHELPS
    M.A. b. at Haverhill, Mass., Sept. 16, 1832. m. Lawyer.
    District Attorney of City of New York. d. 1880.

HENRY CORNELIUS ROBINSON   *Hartford, Conn.*
    M.A., LL.D. b. at Hartford, Conn., Aug. 28, 1832. m.
    Lawyer. Mayor of Hartford.

GEORGE SHIRAS   *Washington, D. C.*
    LL.D. b. at Pittsburg, Pa., Jan. 26, 1833. m. Justice
    of U. S. Supreme Court.

JOEL SUMNER SMITH   *New Haven, Conn.*
    b. at Paxton, Mass., Sept. 11, 1830. m. Asst. Librarian
    at Yale.

KINSLEY TWINING   *Morristown, N. J.*
    D.D., L.H.D. Hamilton. b. at West Point, N. Y., July
    18, 1832. m. Minister. Literary Editor of "The Independent."

GEORGE HENRY WATROUS
    LL.B. b. at Bridgewater, Pa., April 26, 1829. m. Lawyer. R. R. President. Member of Conn. Leg. d. 1889.

JAMES MORRIS WHITON   *New York City.*
    Ph.D. b. at Boston, Mass., April 11, 1833. m. Minister.

CHARLES HENRY WHITTELSEY
    M.A. b. at New Haven, Conn., Oct. 2, 1832. Captain in
    Army in Civil War. Brevet Brigadier-general. d.
    1871.

ANDREW JACKSON WILLARD   *Burlington, Vt.*
  M.D. U. of Vt.   b. at Harvard, Mass., March 19, 1832.
  m. Minister. Physician.

1854

ABRAM ELISHA BALDWIN
  b. at Goshen, Conn., Nov. 18, 1830. m. Minister. d.
  1886.

CHARLES HENRY BARRETT
  M.A., M.D. Harv. b. at Rutland, Vt., May 13, 1833. m.
  Physician. d. 1869.

BENNET JASON BRISTOL   *Webster Groves, Mo.*
  M.D. L. I. Coll. Hos. b. at Naugatuck, Conn., Sept. 15,
  1833. m. Physician.

HORATIO WOODWARD BROWN   *Wooster, O.*
  M.A. b. at Buffalo, N. Y., July 27, 1833. m. Minister.

EDWARD PAYSON BUFFETT   ·   *Jersey City, N. J.*
  M.A., M.D. P. and S. b. at Smithtown, N. Y., Nov. 7,
  1833. m. Physician.

CARROLL CUTLER
  M.A. W. Reserve, D.D. Marietta. b. at Windham, N. H.,
  Jan. 31, 1829. m. Minister. Professor. President of
  Western Reserve College. Author of a work on Ethics,
  etc. d. 1894.

ERASTUS LYMAN DEFOREST
  Ph.B., M.A. b. at Watertown, Conn., June 27, 1834.
  Teacher. Author of mathematical treatises. d. 1888.

CHARLES ANALDO DUPEE   *Chicago, Ill.*
  M.A. b. at West Brookfield, Mass., May 22, 1831. m.
  Teacher. Lawyer.

WILLIAM REED EASTMAN   *Albany, N. Y.*
  M.A. b. at New York City, Oct. 19, 1835. m. Civil
  Engineer. Minister. State Inspector of Public Libraries
  of N. Y. Chaplain in Civil War.

WILLIAM HENRY FENN   *Portland, Me.*
  D.D. b. at Charleston, S. C., March 1, 1834. m. Minister.

WILLARD CUTTING FLAGG
M.A. b. at Moro, Ill., Sept. 16, 1829. m. Farmer.
Letters. U. S. Collector of Internal Revenue. Author
of agricultural and political treatises. d. 1878.

LEWIS WHITMARSH FORD   *Cleveland, O.*
b. at Cummington, Mass., Dec. 12, 1830. m. Lawyer.

SAMUEL CHESTER GALE   *Minneapolis, Minn.*
b. at Royalston, Mass., Sept. 15, 1827. m. Lawyer.
Business.

AUGUSTUS STEBBINS HITCHCOCK   *Plainville, Conn.*
b. at Gt. Barrington, Mass., March 23, 1827. m. Lawyer.

JAMES WILLIAM HUSTED
M.A. b. at Bedford, N. Y., Oct. 31, 1833. m. Teacher.
Lawyer. Business. Member of N. Y. Leg. d. 1892.

WILLIAM HUTCHISON
M.A. b. at Philadelphia, Pa., Sept. 20, 1827. m. Missionary. Teacher. d. 1885.

JAMES KITTREDGE LOMBARD
M.A. b. at Burlington, N. Y., Jan. 15, 1832. m. Teacher.
Minister. d. 1889.

GEORGE DEFOREST LORD
M.A. b. at New York City, Nov. 21, 1833. m. Lawyer.
d. 1892.

GEORGE FREDERICK NICHOLS
b. at Fairfield, Conn., March 8, 1832. Teacher. Lawyer.
d. 1864.

STARR HOYT NICHOLS   *New York City.*
b. at Bethel, Conn., Nov. 16, 1834. m. Minister. Broker.
U. S. Vice Consul at Bremen. Editor of "Social
Economist."

WILLIAM HENRY NORRIS   *Minneapolis, Minn.*
b. at Hallowell, Me., July 24, 1832. m. Lawyer.

LEANDER HUBBELL POTTER
b. at Rockford, Ill. March 15, 1829. m. Teacher. College Professor. d. 1879.

LEMUEL STOUGHTON POTWIN   *Cleveland, O.*
   M.A., D.D. b. at East Windsor, Conn., Feb. 4, 1832.
   m. Teacher. Minister. Professor.

THOMAS GARDINER RITCH   *Stamford, Conn.*
   M.A. b. at North Salem, N. Y., Sept. 18, 1833. m.
   Lawyer.

FRANCIS HENRY SLADE
   b. at Boston, Mass., Sept. 19, 1833. m. Business. d. 1890.

JOSEPH MORGAN SMITH
   b. at Gt. Falls, N. H., April 26, 1833. m. Teacher.
   Minister. d. 1883.

ORSON COWLES SPARROW
   Ph.D., M.D. L. I. Coll. Hos. b. at Killingly, Conn.,
   Sept. 3, 1832. m. Teacher. Physician. d. 1877.

JOHN TAIT   *Meriden, Conn.*
   b. at Trumbull, Conn., Feb. 16, 1828. m. Physician.

CHARLES EDWARD TRUMBULL
   b. at Stonington, Conn., Oct. 31, 1832. d. 1856.

ALEXANDER STEVENSON TWOMBLY   *Newton, Mass.*
   M.A., D.D. b. at Boston, Mass., March 14, 1832. m.
   Minister. Publishing business.

SAMUEL WALKER
   M.A. b. at Londonderry, Pa., June 25, 1825. U. S. Coast
   Survey. Lawyer. Mayor. Judge. Legislator. d. 1881.

EDWARD PAYSON WHITNEY
   M.A. b. at Northampton, Mass., May 22, 1833. Teacher.

ELIZUR WOLCOTT
   M.A. b. at Tallmadge, O., July 14, 1833. m. Teacher.
   Farmer. d. 1873.

1855

WILLIAM DEWITT ALEXANDER   *Honolulu, H. I.*
   M.A. b. at Honolulu, April 2, 1833. m. Teacher. Sur-
   veyor General of H. I. Member of the Privy Council
   of State, 1887. Pres. of Oahu Coll. Author of treatises
   on Hawaiian subjects.

CHARLES JAMES FOX ALLEN   *Louisville, Ky.*
   LL.B. Harv.   b. at Boston, Mass., Aug. 14, 1834.   m.
   Business.

LYMAN DENNISON BREWSTER   *Danbury, Conn.*
   M.A. b. at Salisbury, Conn., July 31, 1832. m. Lawyer.
   Probate Judge.   Judge of Court of Common Pleas.
   Member of Conn. Leg.

NATHANIEL WILLIS BUMSTEAD   *Boston, Mass.*
   M.A. b. at Boston, Mass., March 19, 1834. Teacher.
   Business.

HENRY TREAT CHITTENDEN   *Columbus, O.*
   b. at Columbus, O., Dec. 18, 1834. Lawyer. Editor.
   U. S. Commissioner.

STERNE CHITTENDEN
   b. at Columbus, O., Jan. 1, 1833. m. Lawyer. Letters.
   d. 1887.

HENRY NITCHIE COBB   *New York City.*
   M.A., D.D. Rutgers. b. at New York City, Nov. 15,
   1834. m. Minister. Missionary. Secretary of Board
   of Foreign Missions of Reformed Church.

WILLIAM MASON GROSVENOR
   b. at Ashfield, Mass., April 23, 1835.   Newspaper business.

JOSIAH WILLIAM HARMER
   M.A. LL.B. b. at Philadelphia, Pa., Nov. 23, 1834. Lawyer. d. 1867.

JOHN RODOLPH JARBOE
   M.A. b. at Elk Ridge, Md., Feb. 16, 1836. m. Lawyer.
   d. 1893.

GEORGE ALVAH KITTREDGE   *Boston, Mass.*
   M.A. b. at Boston, Mass., March 29, 1833. Business.
   Vice Consul in Bombay, India.

THEODORE LYMAN   *Hartford, Conn.*
   b. at Hartford, Conn., Jan. 4, 1834. m. Lawyer.

ALFRED BOLIVAR MILLER   *New Haven, Conn.*
   M.A. b. at Chenango, N. Y., April 3, 1831. m. Teacher.

JOHN LAWRENCE MILLS   *Marietta, O.*
   M.A. b. at Norfolk, Conn., Sept. 18, 1832. m. Teacher.
   Minister. Merchant.

FREDERICK WEBSTER OSBORN   *Brooklyn, N. Y.*
M.A. b. at Newark, N. J., Feb. 19, 1834. Minister.
Teacher.

CHARLES RAY PALMER   *New Haven, Conn.*
M.A., D.D. b. at New Haven, Conn., May 2, 1834. m.
Minister. Member of Yale Corporation.

JOHN CALDWELL PARSONS
M.A. b. at Hartford, Conn., June 3, 1832. m. Lawyer.
Business. Bank President. d. 1898.

HENRY RICHMOND SLACK
b. at Plaquemine, La., Oct. 20, 1835. m. Planter.
Farmer. d. 1890.

OSCAR MOSES SMITH   *Hawley, Minn.*
M.A. b. at Java, N. Y., Dec. 20, 1828. m. Minister.

EMIL SPANIER
M.A. b. at Hanover, Germany, April, 1836. Business.
Letters. d. 1872.

CHARLES PIERCE STETSON   *Bangor, Me.*
b. at Bangor, Me., May 24, 1835. m. Lawyer.

GEORGE STUART
b. at Sherman, Conn., Oct. 24, 1832. In Army in Civil
War. d. 1863.

GEORGE TALCOTT
b. at West Hartford, Conn., Jan. 8, 1833. m. Lawyer.
Business. d. 1871.

JOHN EDWARDS TODD   *Riverside, Cal.*
M.A., D.D. b. at Northampton, Mass., Dec. 6, 1833. m.
Minister.

LUTHER HENRY TUCKER
M.A. b. at Rochester, N. Y., Oct. 19, 1834. m. Editor.
Publisher. d. 1897.

CHARLES MELLEN TYLER   *Ithaca, N. Y.*
M.A., D.D. b. at Limington, Me., Jan. 8, 1831. m.
Minister. Professor at Cornell. Author of philosophical works; "Grounds of Religious Belief, Historical
and Philosophical."

WILLIAM WHEELER
M.A., LL.B. Harv. b. at New York City, Aug. 14, 1836.
Lawyer. In Army in Civil War. d. 1864.

PATRICK HENRY WOODWARD   *Hartford, Conn.*
b. at Franklin, Conn., March 19, 1833. m. Newspaper
business. P. O. Dept. Sec'y of Hartford Board of Trade.
Author of historical treatises, etc.

WILLIAM CUTLER WYMAN   *Brooklyn, N. Y.*
M.A. b. at Brooklyn, N. Y., April 7, 1834. m. Teacher.
Minister. Business.

HENRY ALBERT YARDLEY
M.A. b. at Philadelphia, Pa., Dec. 20, 1834. m. Teacher.
Minister. Professor. d. 1882.

1856

NELSON BARTHOLOMEW
b. at Hardwick, Mass., Dec. 29, 1834. Lawyer. In Army
in Civil War. d. 1861.

DAVID JOSIAH BREWER   *Washington, D. C.*
M.A., LL.D. and Iowa U. and Washburn. b. at Smyrna,
Asia Minor, June 20, 1837. m. Justice of U. S. Supreme
Court. Member of U. S. Venezuelan Commission.

HENRY BILLINGS BROWN   *Washington, D. C.*
LL.D. and Michigan. b. in Berkshire Co., Mass., March 2,
1836. m. Justice of U. S. Supreme Court.

CHARLES EDWIN BULKLEY
b. at Colchester, Conn., Dec. 19, 1835. Lawyer. In
Army in Civil War. d. 1864.

WOLCOTT CALKINS   *Kansas City, Mo.*
D.D. Hamilton. b. at Corning, N. Y., June 10, 1831. m.
Teacher. Minister.

WILLIAM HARVEY WILLSON CAMPBELL
b. at Boston, Mass., Oct. 23, 1833. m. Editor. Foreign
Agent. d. 1892.

ARTHUR DICKINSON   *Richmond, Va.*
b. at Macon, Ga., July, 1835. m. Lawyer.

CHARLES EDWARD FELLOWES   *Hartford, Conn.*
b. at Hartford, Conn., June 17, 1834. m. Lawyer.

LUKE WILLIAM FINLAY   *Memphis, Tenn.*
b. near Brandon, Miss., Oct. 8, 1831. m. Lawyer.
Lieutenant Colonel in Confederate Army.

LOUIS CHRISTOPHER FISCHER   *Baltimore, Md.*
b. at Baltimore, Md., Aug. 13, 1834. m. Lawyer. Bank
Officer.

WILLIAM JAMES HARRIS   *Nashua, N. H.*
M.A., D.D. Trinity. b. at West Brattleboro, Vt., May 21,
1834. m. Minister. Archdeacon of Diocese of Vermont.

WILBUR JOHNSON   *Brooklyn, Conn.*
b. at Genoa, N. Y., March 1, 1831. m. Minister.

SENECA MCNEIL KEELER   *Newton Center, Mass.*
M.A. b. at West Newbury, Mass., May 31, 1835. m.
Minister.

BENJAMIN DRAKE MAGRUDER   *Chicago, Ill.*
b. in Jefferson Co., Miss., Sept. 27, 1838. m. Lawyer.
Judge. Chief Justice of Supreme Court of Illinois.

CHARLES ADDISON MANN
b. at Utica, N. Y., May 29, 1835. m. Lawyer. Capitalist.
d. 1896.

JOHN MONTEITH   *Sausalito, Cal.*
M.A. b. at Elyria, O., Jan. 31, 1833. m. Minister. Lecturer. Author. Author of books on Natural History,
etc.

LEWIS RICHARD PACKARD
M.A., Ph.D. b. at Philadelphia, Pa., Aug. 22, 1836. m.
Professor of Greek at Yale. Vice President of American
Philological Society. d. 1884.

LEVI LEONARD PAINE   *Bangor, Me.*
M.A., D.D. b. at East Randolph, Mass., Oct. 10, 1832. m.
Professor of Church History.

HENRY EDWARDS PARDEE
M.A. b. at Trumbull, Conn., Aug. 11, 1831. m. Lawyer.
Judge. d. 1889.

JAMES LYMAN RACKLEFF   *Portland, Me.*
 M.A. b. at Portland, Me., Feb. 9, 1836. m. Lawyer.

GEORGE CHESTER ROBINSON
 b. at Hartwick, N. Y., Aug. 9, 1833. m. Minister. d. 1863.

EDWARD ALFRED SMITH
 M.A. b. at East Woodstock, Conn., July 22, 1835. m.
 Minister. Member of Yale Corporation. d. 1895.

OLIVER STARR TAYLOR
 b. at Brookfield, Conn., March 13, 1832. m. Minister.
 d. 1874.

EDWARD CORNELIUS TOWNE   *Oak Park, Ill.*
 b. at Goshen, Mass., Oct. 9, 1834. m. Minister. Author.
 Newspaper Editor.

EDWARD ASHLEY WALKER
 M.A. b. at New Haven, Conn., Nov. 24, 1834. m. Minister. d. 1866.

BENJAMIN WEBB   *New York City.*
 M.A. b. at New York City, July 30, 1831. Minister.

JAMES LYMAN WHITNEY   *Boston, Mass.*
 M.A. b. at Northampton, Mass., Nov. 28, 1835. In
 Boston Public Library.

TIMOTHY KEELER WILCOX
 M.A. b. at North Greenwich, Conn., May 18, 1835.
 Minister. d. 1863.

AHAB GEORGE WILKINSON   *Washington, D. C.*
 M.A. and Ph.D. Columbian U. b. at Willimantic, Conn.,
 Feb. 22, 1834. m. Chief Examiner in U. S. Patent Office.

EDWARD FRANKLIN WILLIAMS   *Chicago, Ill.*
 M.A., D.D. Illinois. b. at Uxbridge, Mass., July 22, 1832.
 m. Minister. Editor of "The Congregationalist."

SAMUEL FAY WOODS
 M.A. b. at Barre, Mass., June 23, 1837. Lawyer. In
 Army in Civil War. d. 1864.

JOHN HUNTER WORRALL
 M.A., Ph.D. b. at Delaware Co., Pa., Feb. 18, 1827.
 Teacher. d. 1892.

1857

EDMUND THOMPSON ALLEN   *St. Louis, Mo.*
    M.A. b. at Fair Haven, Mass., Aug. 10, 1836. m. Lawyer. Business.

ORRIN FRINK AVERY
    b. in Susquehannah Co., Pa., May 1, 1831. m. Lawyer. d. 1870.

LESTER BRADNER   *Dansville, N. Y.*
    b. at Dansville, N. Y., Nov. 1, 1836. R. R. business.

JOSEPH PAYSON BUCKLAND
    b. at Springfield, Mass., Oct. 7, 1835. m. Lawyer d. 1879.

FRANCIS EUGENE BUTLER
    M.A. b. at Suffield, Conn., Feb. 7, 1825. Minister. Chaplain in Civil War. d. 1863.

JOSEPH ALONZO CHRISTMAN
    LL.B. Louisville. b. at Evansburg, Pa., Oct. 25, 1854. Lawyer. Banker. d. 1888.

JOHN CALVIN DAY   *Hartford, Conn.*
    M.A. b. at Hartford, Conn., Nov. 3, 1835. m. Lawyer.

HENRY SWIFT DEFOREST
    M.A., D.D. Beloit. b. at South Edmeston, N. Y., March 17, 1833. m. Teacher. Minister. President of Talladega College. d. 1896.

SOLOMON JOHNSON DOUGLASS   *New Haven, Conn.*
    b. at New Hartford, Conn., Oct. 3, 1834. m. Minister.

SAMUEL MARTIN FREELAND   *Pueblo, Col.*
    M.A. b. at Philadelphia, Pa., Nov. 23, 1831. m. Teacher. Minister.

GEORGE SEAMAN GRAY
    M.A. b. at New York City, July 10, 1835. m. Minister. Business. d. 1885.

JAMES PAYNE GREEN   *Church Hill, Miss.*
    b. in Jefferson Co., Miss., Jan. 7, 1837. m. Teacher. Planter.

ALFRED HAND   *Scranton, Pa.*
M.A. b. at Honesdale, Pa., March 26, 1835. m. Lawyer.
Judge of Supreme Court of Pa.

VOLNEY HICKOX
M.A. b. at Rutland, N. Y., Nov. 1, 1836. m. Newspaper Correspondent. d. 1898.

LEVI HOLBROOK   *New York City.*
M.A. b. at Westborough, Mass., March 7, 1836. m.
Business. Travelling. Letters.

STEPHEN HOLDEN   *Sherburne, N. Y.*
b. at So. Hartwick, N. Y., April 26, 1832. m. Lawyer.

JOHN MILTON HOLMES
b. in Kent, Eng., May 20, 1832. m. Minister. d. 1871.

JAMES WAKEMAN HUBBELL
M.A., D.D. Marietta. b. at Wilton, Conn., March 29,
1835. m. Minister. d. 1896.

WILLIAM EDWARD HULBERT   *Cromwell, Conn.*
M.A. b. at Middletown, Conn., May 19, 1834. Business.

HENRY STRONG HUNTINGTON   *Milton, Mass.*
M.A. b. at New York City, July 18, 1836. m. Teacher.
Minister.

JOSEPH COOKE JACKSON   *New York City.*
M.A., LL.B. U. C. N. Y. and Harv. b. at Newark, N. J.,
Aug. 5, 1835. m. Lawyer. Brevet Brigadier-General.

HENRY PORTER McCOY
b. at North Haven, Conn., May 7, 1830. m. Teacher. d.
1860.

ALMON BAXTER MERWIN   *Brooklyn, N. Y.*
M.A. b. at Brooklyn, N. Y., June 27, 1835. m. Teacher.

GEORGE AUGUSTUS NOLEN
M.A. b. at Sutton, Mass., Jan. 9, 1831. Tutor at Yale.
Ass't Examiner in U. S. Patent Office. d. 1875.

CYRUS NORTHROP   *Minneapolis, Minn.*
LL.B., LL.D. b. at Ridgefield, Conn., Sept. 30, 1834. m.
Professor of English at Yale. President of University of
Minn.

DAVID GUSTAVUS PORTER   *Waterbury, Conn.*
  b. at Waterbury, Conn., March 8, 1833.   Teacher.   Letters.

MICHAEL WALLER ROBINSON   *Chicago, Ill.*
  b. in Callaway Co., Mo., Oct. 13, 1837.   m.   Lawyer.
  Member of Ill. Leg.

EDSON ROGERS   *Cincinnatus, N. Y.*
  M.A.   b. at Whitney's Point, N. Y., May 22, 1833.   m.
  Minister.   Teacher.

WILLIAM HENRY SAVARY   *South Boston, Mass.*
  b. at Groveland, Mass., April 18, 1835.   m.   Minister.

WILDER SMITH
  M.A.   b. at Boston, Mass., July 17, 1835.   m.   Minister.
  Author of "Extempore Preaching."   d. 1891.

AUGUSTUS HOPKINS STRONG   *Rochester, N. Y.*
  D.D. and Brown, LL.D. Bucknell.   b. at Rochester, N. Y.,
  Aug. 3, 1836.   m.   Minister.   President of Rochester
  Theol. Seminary.   Author of "Systematic Theology,"
  "Philosophy and Religion."

GEORGE TUCKER   *Bermuda.*
  M.A. and Trinity.   b. at Bermuda, 1837.   m.   Minister.

MOSES COIT TYLER   *Ithaca, N. Y.*
  M.A., LL.D. Wooster, L.H.D. Col.   b. at Griswold,
  Conn., Aug. 2, 1835.   m.   Minister.   Professor of Eng-
  lish at U. of Mich.   Professor of American History and
  Literature at Cornell.   Author of History of American
  Lit.; a Manual of Eng. Lit.

NATHAN DANA WELLS   *Brooklyn, N. Y.*
  b. at Northfield, N. H., June 17, 1831.   m.   Lawyer.

ARTHUR MARTIN WHEELER   *New Haven, Conn.*
  M.A., LL.D.   b. at Weston, Conn., June 21, 1835.   m.
  Professor of History at Yale.

1858

MONTELIUS ABBOTT
  M.A., LL.B. U. of P.   b. at Philadelphia, Pa., Nov. 2,
  1838.   Lawyer.   d. 1877.

JOHN TAYLOR BAIRD
    M.A., D.D. Omaha. b. at Cincinnati, O., Dec. 3, 1834.
    m. Minister.

EDWARD PAYSON BATCHELOR
    LL.B. Harv., M.A. b. at Whitinsville, Mass., Jan. 30,
    1835. Lawyer. d. 1876.

SAMUEL CALDWELL
    b. at Salem, Pa., April 14, 1834. m. Lawyer. Acting
    Ass't Adj. General in Civil War. d. 1872.

ISAAC DELANO
    M.A., LL.B. U. of Mich. b. at Fair Haven, Mass., Oct.
    27, 1833. m. Business. Lawyer.

LOUIS DEMBINSKI
    M.A. b. at Tarnow, Galicia, Nov. 25, 1828. m. Teacher.
    Business. d. 1886.

EDWARD THOMAS ELLIOT   *Minneapolis, Minn.*
    M.A., LL.B. Harv. b. at Towanda, Pa., Jan. 26, 1837. m.
    Lawyer. Business.

CHARLES MERWIN FENN
    Physician.

DELANCY FREEBORN
    LL.B. Albany. b. at Knoxville, Pa., Sept. 9, 1833. m.
    Teacher. Reporter. Business.

JOSIAH WILLARD GIBBS   *New Haven, Conn.*
    M.A., Ph.D. and Erlangen, LL.D. Williams and Princeton.
    b. at New Haven, Conn., Feb. 11, 1839. m. Professor of
    Mathematical Physics at Yale. Foreign Member of Royal
    Society of London. Member of Nat'l Academy of
    Sciences, Washington, and other Scientific Societies.
    Author of books on Mathematics and Physics.

ROBERT CHANDLER HASKELL
    M.A. b. at Weathersfield, Vt., Sept. 6, 1834. m. Teacher.
    Business. d. 1897.

EDGAR LAING HEERMANCE
    M.A. b. at New York City, April 30, 1833. m. Minister.
    d. 1888.

ARTHUR NELSON HOLLISTER
M.A. b. at Andover, Conn., Dec. 28, 1835. m. Teacher.
Insurance. d. 1897.

AUGUSTUS TURNER JONES   *Brockton, Mass.*
M.A. b. at North Bridgewater, Mass., May 21, 1832. m.
Teacher. Editor. Business.

CHAUNCEY SEYMOUR KELLOGG   *McComb, Miss.*
b. at Woodville, Miss., Sept. 12, 1837. m. Planter.
Teacher.

WILLIAM ALLEN LANE   *Fort Worth, Texas.*
b. at Gorham, Me., Dec. 4, 1839. m. Business.

SAMUEL HENRY LEE   *Springfield, Mass.*
M.A. b. at Lisbon, Conn., Dec. 21, 1832. m. Teacher.
Minister.

GEORGE BOARDMAN McCLELLAN   *Jacksonville, Fla.*
M.A. b. in King and Queen Co., Va., July 27, 1833. m.
Teacher. In Confederate Army in Civil War.

WILLIAM ALLEN McDOWELL
M.A. b. at Allenville, Pa., July 15, 1828. m. Teacher.
Lawyer. Editor. d. 1897.

EDWARD AUGUSTUS MANICE
Ph.B., M.A., LL.B. Col. b. at New York City, Oct. 19,
1838. m. Lawyer. d. 1877.

ARTHUR MATHEWSON   *New York City.*
M.A., M.D. U. C. N. Y. b. at Brooklyn, Conn., Sept. 11,
1837. Surgeon in Brooklyn Eye and Ear Hospital.
Member of many scientific societies of his profession.
Author of treatises on diseases of eye and ear.

DANIEL AUGUSTUS MILES
M.A. b. at Rutland, Mass., April 2, 1835. Minister. d.
1895.

HENRY ANDREWS PRATT
LL.B. Columbian U. b. at Waterbury, Conn., Aug. 27,
1833. m. Teacher. d. 1896.

EBEN GREENOUGH SCOTT   *Wilkes-Barre, Pa.*
b. at Wilkes-Barre. June 15, 1836. m. Lawyer. Author.

EDWARD SEYMOUR
M.A. b. at Bloomfield, N. J., April 1, 1835. m. Editor. Publisher. d. 1877.

FREDERICK WILLIAM STEVENS   *New York City.*
LL.B. Col. b. at New York City, Sept. 19, 1839. m. Lawyer. Business.

HENRY EDWARDS SWEETSER
b. at New York City, Feb. 19, 1837. Editor of New York World. d. 1870.

ELISHA SMITH THOMAS
M.A., D.D. b. at Wickford, R. I., March 2, 1834. m. Teacher. Minister. Bishop of Kansas. d. 1895.

HENRY HOLMES TURNER
b. at Quincy, Ill., Oct. 31, 1831. Business. d. 1893.

THOMAS GILBERT VALPEY
M.A. and Trinity. b. at Andover, Mass., July 16, 1832. Teacher. d. 1890.

ADDISON VAN NAME   *New Haven, Conn.*
M.A. b. at Fenton, N. Y., Nov. 15, 1835. m. Librarian of Yale University.

1859

WILLIAM HENRY ANDERSON   *Lowell, Mass.*
b. at Londonderry, N. H., Jan. 12, 1836. Lawyer.

THOMAS CHALMERS BRAINERD   *Montreal, Canada.*
b. at Philadelphia, Pa., Sept. 27, 1837. m. Business. Member of British Ass'n for Advancement of Science.

LOUIS HENRY BRISTOL   *New Haven, Conn.*
b. at New Haven, Conn., Dec. 14, 1838. Lawyer.

ROBERT JOHN CARPENTER
M.A. b. at Demorestville, Canada, Oct. 13, 1837. m. Business. d. 1889.

EDWARD CARRINGTON
LL.B. Col. b. at Hartford, Conn., Feb. 15, 1838. Lawyer. In Army in Civil War. d. 1865.

3

HASKET DERBY CATLIN *Eastport, Me.*
M.A. b. at Staten Island, N. Y., June 26, 1839. m. Minister.

JOSEPH ALDRICH COOPER *Edinboro, Pa.*
M.A. b. at Mattituck, N. Y., Aug. 27, 1834. m. Teacher.

THOMAS BRADFORD DWIGHT
b. at Portland, Me., Sept. 17, 1837. m. Lawyer. d. 1877.

LESTER BRADNER FAULKNER
b. at Dansville, N. Y., April 4, 1837. m. Lawyer. d. 1890.

SAMUEL DORR FAULKNER
b. at Dansville, N. Y., Nov. 14, 1835. Lawyer. Business. d. 1878.

GILBERT OTIS FAY *Hartford, Conn.*
M.A., Ph.D. W. Reserve. b. at Wadsworth, O., Nov. 8, 1834. m. Instructor in the American School for the Deaf.

WILLIAM PIERCE FREEMAN *Champion, N. Y.*
b. at Champion, N. Y., Dec. 20, 1833. Farmer.

CHARLES HEEBNER GROSS *Philadelphia, Pa.*
b. at Trappe, Pa., May 9, 1838. Lawyer.

BURTON NORVELL HARRISON *New York City.*
b. at New Orleans, La., July 6, 1838. m. Lawyer. Private Sec'y to Jefferson Davis during Civil War.

SAMUEL SLAWSON HARTWELL
M.A. Minisink, N. Y., Nov. 30, 1831. m. Teacher. d. 1883.

JOHN HASKELL HEWITT *Williamstown, Mass.*
M.A. and Williams. b. at Preston, Conn., Aug. 8, 1835. m. Professor of Ancient Languages at Williams College.

GEORGE WILLIAM JONES *Ithaca, N. Y.*
M.A. b. at East Corinth, Me., Oct. 14, 1837. m. Professor of Mathematics at Cornell.

THOMAS RAYNESFORD LOUNSBURY *New Haven, Conn.*
M.A., LL.D. and Harv. b. at Ovid, N. Y., Jan. 1, 1838. Professor of English at Yale.

HOMER GEORGE NEWTON   *Sherburne, N. Y.*
M.A., M.D. U. C. N. Y. b. at Sherburne, N. Y., Oct. 25,
1835. m. Eye and ear Surgeon. Bank Official. Member of American Opthalmological and Ontological Societies, etc.

SAMUEL DAVIS PAGE   *Philadelphia, Pa.*
b. at Philadelphia, Pa., Sept. 22, 1840. m. Lawyer. Sub-treasurer of U. S.

WILLIAM HENRY RICE   *New Dorp, N. Y.*
M.A. b. at Bethlehem, Pa., Sept. 8, 1840. Minister.

EUGENE SCHUYLER
Ph.D., LL.B. Col., LL.D. and Williams. b. at Ithaca, N. Y.,
Feb. 26, 1840. m. Lawyer. Letters. U. S. Minister to
Roumania, Servia and Greece. Member of Historical
and Geographical Societies. Translator and editor of
Russian books. d. 1890.

EUGENE SMITH   *New York City.*
LL.B. Albany.   b. at New York City, April, 1836.
m. Lawyer.

ROBERT STILES   *Richmond, Va.*
b. in Kentucky, June 27, 1836. m. Lawyer.

WILLIAM AUGUSTUS STILES
b. at Deckerstown, N. J., March 9, 1837. Editor of " Garden and Forest." Park Commissioner of N. Y. City.
d. 1897.

HEZEKIAH WATKINS
LL.B. Albany. b. at Liberty, N. Y., Aug. 1835. m.
Railroad official. Gov't Inspector of Northern Pacific
R. R. d. 1884.

GEORGE PHILIP WELLES   *Chicago, Ill.*
M.A. b. at Wethersfield, Conn., Feb. 21, 1838. Teacher.

HENRY JUDSON WHEELER
b. at West Bloomfield, N. J., Nov. 1836. d. 1858.

ASHER HENRY WILCOX   *Norwich, Conn.*
b. at Norwich, Conn., Nov. 16, 1837. m. Minister.

HENRY WINN   *Boston, Mass.*
b. at Whitingham, Conn., Dec. 8, 1837. m. Lawyer.
Business. Member of Mass. Leg.

ARTHUR BURR WOOD
    LL.B. Albany.   b. at Middletown, N. Y., 1837.   U. S. Consul and Consular Inspector.   d. 1895.

ARTHUR WILLIAMS WRIGHT   *New Haven, Conn.*
    Ph.D.   b. at Lebanon, Conn., Sept. 8, 1836.   m.   Professor of Experimental Physics at Yale.

1860

ALONZO BRAYTON BALL   *New York City.*
    M.D. Col.   b. at New York City, Feb. 10, 1840.   Physician. Visiting Physician to Bellevue and St. Luke's Hospitals. Lecturer at P. and S.

GEORGE LOUIS BEERS   *Topeka, Kan.*
    M.A., M.D. Col.   b. at Stratford, Conn., Dec. 28, 1839. Physician.

LINUS BLAKESLEY   *Topeka, Kan.*
    D.D.   b. at Terryville, Conn., Dec. 16, 1837.   Minister.

CHARLES ALFRED BOIES
    b. at Boston, Mass., June 3, 1838.   Minister.   d.   1863.

EDWARD BOLTWOOD
    b. at Amherst, Mass., Sept. 4, 1839.   m.   Lawyer.   Insurance business.   d. 1878.

HENRY WARD CAMP
    b. at Hartford, Conn., Feb. 4, 1839.   Major in Army in Civil War.   d. 1864.

OSCAR MORTIMER CARRIER
    M.A.   b. at Conquest, N. Y., Aug. 2, 1835.   m.   Prof. of Latin at Olivet College.   d. 1865.

JOSEPH LEONARD DANIELS   *Olivet, Mich.*
    D.D.   b. at East Medway, Mass., Aug. 1, 1833.   m.   Prof. of Greek in Olivet College.

LOWNDES HENRY DAVIS   *Jackson, Mo.*
    LL.B. Louisville.   b. at Jackson, Mo., Dec. 14, 1836.   m. Lawyer.   Member of Congress.

ROBERT STEWART DAVIS   *Philadelphia, Pa.*
    b. at Philadelphia, Pa., April 23, 1838.   m.   Editor.

FRANCIS DELAFIELD   *New York City.*
    M.D. Col., LL.D.   b. at New York City, Aug. 3, 1841.   m.
    Professor of Pathology and Practical Medicine in P. and
    S.   Author of "A Handbook of Pathological Anatomy,"
    "A Manual of Physical Diagnosis," "Studies in Patholog-
    ical Anatomy."

DANIEL CADY EATON   *New Haven, Conn.*
    LL.B. Albany.   b. at Johnstown, N. Y., June 16, 1837.   m.
    Writer and Lecturer on subjects relating to art and edu-
    cation.   Professor of the History and Criticism of Art at
    Yale.   Author of a "Handbook to Greek and Roman
    Sculpture," etc.

WILLIAM FOWLER
    LL.B. Albany.   b. at Albany, N. Y., Sept. 23, 1839.   Law-
    yer.   d. 1874.

WILLIAM HENRY HALE   *Brooklyn, N. Y.*
    LL.B. Albany, M.A., Ph.D.   b. at Albany, N. Y., Aug. 20,
    1840.   Lawyer.   Business.

HENRY LEWIS HALL
    b. at Guilford, Conn., Nov. 26, 1836.   m.   Minister.   d.
    1869.

THOMAS GORDON HUNT
    b. at New Bedford, Mass., July 29, 1838.   m.   Business.
    d. 1891.

WILLIAM HENRY HURLBUT   *New York City.*
    M.A.   b. at New York City, June 17, 1840.   m.   Business.

MARCUS PERRIN KNOWLTON   *Springfield, Mass.*
    LL.D.   b. at Wilbraham, Mass., Feb. 3, 1839.   m.   Lawyer.
    Judge of Mass. Superior Court.

OTHNIEL CHARLES MARSH   *New Haven, Conn.*
    M.A., Ph.D. Heidelberg, LL.D. Harv.   b. at Lockport,
    N. Y., Oct. 29, 1831.   Prof. of Palæontology at Yale.
    President Nat'l Academy of Sciences.   U. S. Palæontolo-
    gist.   Member of several foreign academies of science.
    Author of numerous works on his subject.

WILLIAM WISNER MARTIN
    b. at Rahway, N. J., Dec. 18, 1837.   m.   Minister.   d.
    1865.

EDWARD GAY MASON   *Chicago, Ill.*
M.A., LL.D. Knox. b. at Bridgeport, Conn., Aug. 23,
1839. m. Lawyer. Member of Yale Corporation.

JOHN MOSES MORRIS
b. at Wethersfield, Conn., April 27, 1837. m. Editor.
Clerk of U. S. Senate. d. 1873.

NATHANIEL NORTON   .   *New York City.*
LL.B. Col. b. at Brooklyn, N. Y., Oct. 7, 1839. m.
Manufacturer. Publisher of "American Business Guide."

ALFRED CONRAD PALFREY
b. at Franklin, La., March 20, 1839. m. Lawyer. d. 1879.

WILLIAM PENNINGTON   *Paterson, N. J.*
LL.B. Col. b. at Paterson, N. J., Aug. 27, 1839. Lawyer.

WILLIAM WALTER PHELPS
M.A., LL.B. Col., LL.D. and Rutgers. b. at New York
City, Aug. 24, 1839. m. Lawyer. Member of Congress
and of Yale Corporation. Minister to Austria. Minister
to Germany. d. 1894.

CHARLES HERBERT RICHARDS   *Philadelphia, Pa.*
M.A. D.D. Beloit. b. at Meriden, N. H., March 13, 1839.
m. Minister. Author of "Songs of Christian Praise."
"Scriptural Selections for Responsive Reading," etc.

EUGENE LAMB RICHARDS   *New Haven, Conn.*
M.A. b. at Brooklyn, N. Y., Dec. 27, 1838. m. Professor
of Mathematics at Yale. Author of various works on
mathematics.

JACOB WADSWORTH RUSSELL
b. at Chicago, Ill., Dec. 22, 1839. Sec'y of Chicago Board
of Health. d. 1875.

JAMES HENRY SCHNEIDER
b. in Turkey, March 14, 1839. Teacher. In Army in
Civil War. d. 1864.

WILLIAM THAYER SMITH   *Hanover, N. H.*
M.A., M.D. Dartmouth and U. C. N. Y. b. at New York
City, March 30, 1839. m. Professor of Anatomy and
Physiology at Dartmouth. Author of text book for
schools on Physiology.

JOSEPH LORD TAINTOR
   M.A. b. at Colchester, Conn., Sept. 21, 1835. m. Publisher. d. 1881.

SAMUEL REED WARREN   *Washington, D. C.*
   b. at Wardsborough, Vt., April 1835. Lawyer. Connected with U. S. Bureau of Education.

THOMAS HOWELL WHITE   *New York City.*
   M.D. b. at New Haven, Conn., Feb. 4, 1840. Physician.

LEMUEL TRIPP WILLCOX   *New Bedford, Mass.*
   M.A. b. at Fairhaven, Mass., Aug. 8, 1835. m. Lawyer.

MASON YOUNG   *New York City.*
   M.A., LL.B. Col. b. at Brooklyn, N. Y., May 6, 1838. m. Lawyer. Member of Yale Corporation.

1861

HUBBARD ARNOLD
   M.A. b. at Westfield, Mass., Jan. 5, 1840. Cotton business. d. 1875.

SIMEON EBEN BALDWIN   *New Haven, Conn.*
   M.A., LL.D. Harv. b. at New Haven, Conn., Feb. 5, 1840. m. Lawyer. Prof. of Law at Yale. Judge of Supr. Court of Conn. Pres. American Bar Association. Member of Committee on International Arbitration. Author of numerous articles on legal questions.

GEORGE BUCKINGHAM BEECHER   *Hillsboro, Ohio.*
   b. at Zanesville, O., Sept. 7, 1841. m. Minister.

GEORGE BERNARD BONNEY   *New York City.*
   b. at Rochester, Mass., March 10, 1839. m. Lawyer.

MILTON BULKLEY
   b. at Southport, Conn., July 14, 1840. m. Shipping and commission business. d. 1872.

JAMES GARDNER CLARK   *New Haven, Conn.*
   M.A. b. at Fayetteville, N. Y., Dec. 25, 1835. m. Teacher. Business. Lawyer.

WILLIAM COOK
b. at New York City, April 3, 1842. m. Professor of German at Harvard and Mass. Inst. of Technology. Capt. in Civil War. Brevet Major. Author of a German Grammar; French and English Dictionary. d. 1885.

FRANKLIN BOWDITCH DEXTER *New Haven, Conn.*
M.A. b. at Fair Haven, Mass., Sept. 11, 1842. m. Larned Prof. of History at Yale. Ass't Librarian at Yale. Secretary of the University. Author of "Biographical Sketches of Graduates of Yale College, with Annals of College History."

HENRY REES DURFEE *Palmyra, N. Y.*
M.A., LL.B. Albany Law School. b. at Palmyra, N. Y., Oct. 5, 1840. m. Lawyer. Member of N. Y. Leg.

DAVID WILLIAM EAVES *Lewiston, Idaho.*
M.A., J.U.D. Heidelberg. b. at Social Hill, Ky., July 18, 1838. m. Banker. Real estate business.

WALTER HANFORD *New York City.*
M.A. b. at New York City, Dec. 1, 1840. m. Dry goods business.

JAMES LANMAN HARMAR
M.A. b. at Chester Co., Pa., May 20, 1841. m. Lawyer. d. 1880.

WILLIAM HENRY HIGBEE *New York City.*
M.A. b. at Philadelphia, Pa., Nov. 3, 1839. Business. In Navy in Civil War.

ANTHONY HIGGINS *Wilmington, Del.*
LL.D. b. at St. George's, Del., Oct. 1, 1840. Lawyer. Att'y of U. S. for Dist. of Delaware. Member of Congress.

JAMES NEVINS HYDE *Chicago, Ill.*
M.A., M.D. U. of P. and Rush. b. at Norwich, Conn., June 20, 1840. m. Physician. Prof. at Chicago Med. School. Pres. Amer. Dermatological Ass'n. Editor of Chicago Med. Journal. Asst. surgeon at Washington Hospitals in Civil War.

HENRY NORTON JOHNSON
M.A. b. at Meriden, Conn., July 11, 1831. Principal Hopkins Grammar School. d. 1892.

FRANCIS EDWARD KERNOCHAN
LL.B. Col., M.A. b. at New York City, Dec. 12, 1840.
m. Lawyer. Business. d. 1884.

HARVEY SHELDON KITCHEL *South Bethlehem, Pa.*
M.A. b. at Plymouth Hollow, Conn., Aug. 12, 1839. m.
Railroad business.

CHARLES GRISWOLD GURLEY MERRILL *New Haven, Conn.*
M.D., M.A. b. at Newburyport, Mass., July 27, 1836. m.
U. S. Internal Revenue Service. Surgeon in Civil War.

JOHN HANSON MITCHELL *Port Tobacco, Md.*
M.A. b. at Linden, Md., June 25, 1842. m. Lawyer.

NATHANIEL SCHUYLER MOORE *Winsted, Conn.*
M.A. b. at New York City, Feb. 16, 1839. m. Minister.

DAVID JUDSON OGDEN
B.D. b. at Whitesboro, N. Y., Dec. 24, 1837. Minister.
d. 1891.

CHARLES POMEROY OTIS
M.A., Ph.D. b. at Lebanon, Conn., April 8, 1840. m.
Prof. of Modern Languages at Mass. Institute of Technology. Author of German Grammar; editor and translator of French and German works. d. 1888.

WILLIAM EDWARDS PARK *Gloversville, N. Y.*
D.D. Marietta. b. at Andover, Mass., July 1, 1837. m.
Minister. Author of "Decisive Battles of the World's
History."

EDWARD PHILLIPS PAYSON *Montclair, N. J.*
b. at Fayetteville, N. Y., Mar., 1840. m. Minister. Chaplain in Army in Civil War.

JOHN BARNARD PEARSE *Boston, Mass.*
b. at Philadelphia, Pa., April 19, 1842. m. Patentee.
Iron and steel business.

TRACY PECK *New Haven, Conn.*
M.A. b. at Bristol, Conn., May 24, 1838. m. Prof. of
Latin at Yale. Pres. American Philological Association.
Author of essays on Latin Pronunciation; editor of
"Letters of Younger Pliny."

GEORGE CLAP PERKINS
M.A. b. at Hartford, Conn., Aug. 8, 1839. m. Wire
mattress business. d. 1875.

SYLVESTER FRANKLIN SCHOONMAKER
b. at Albany, N. Y., Nov. 5, 1836. Inventor. Chaplain
in Civil War. d. 1887.

JOSEPH LUCIEN SHIPLEY
b. at Londonderry, N. H., Mar. 31, 1836. m. Newspaper
editor. d. 1894.

GILBERT MILES STOCKING
b. at Waterbury, Conn., Dec. 22, 1838. In Army in Civil
War. d. 1865.

JOHN DRESSER TUCKER   *Hartford, Conn.*
b. at Scotland, Conn., Dec. 19, 1838. m. Lawyer. Paper
business.

1862

FREDERICK ADAMS   *Newark, N. J.*
b. at Amherst, N. H., Oct. 9, 1840. m. Lawyer.

IRA RUSH ALEXANDER
b. at Lewiston, Pa., May 5, 1840. In Army in Civil War.
d. 1863.

JOHN WESLEY ALLING   *New Haven, Conn.*
M.A. b. at Orange, Conn., Oct. 24, 1841. Lawyer.

HENRY SAMUEL BARNUM   *Constantinople, Turkey.*
b. at Stratford, Conn., Aug. 13, 1837. Missionary in Asia
Minor.

GEORGE MILLER BEARD
M.D. P. and S., M.A. b. at Montville, Conn. May 8,
1839. m. Specialist in the treatment of diseases by
electricity. Author of "Medical and Surgical Electricity." d. 1883.

CHARLES FREDERICK BRADLEY
b. at Hudson City, N. J., April 4, 1840. m. Minister. d.
1896.

DANIEL HENRY CHAMBERLAIN   *West Brookfield, Mass.*
LL.B. Harv., LL.D. U. of S. C. b. at West Brookfield,
Mass., June 23, 1835. m. Lawyer. Lecturer. In Army
in Civil War. Governor of South Carolina, '74-'77.

JAMES BALLOCH CHASE   *Correctionville, Iowa.*
b. at Woodstock, Vt., Aug. 12, 1837. m. Minister.

EDWARD BENTON COE   *New York City.*
D.D. and Rutgers. b. at Milford, Conn., June 11, 1842.
m. Prof. of Modern Languages at Yale. Minister.

JAMES HENRY CROSBY   *Bangor, Me.*
b. at Bangor, Me., May 22, 1840. m. Minister.

HEMAN PACKARD DEFOREST   *Detroit, Mich.*
b. at North Bridgewater, Mass., Aug. 20, 1839. m.
Minister.

CHARLES EUSTIS HUBBARD   *Boston, Mass.*
b. at Boston, Mass., Aug. 7, 1842. m. Lawyer.

JOHN WESLEY JOHNSON   *Eugene City, Oregon.*
b. at Kansas City, Mo., March 22, 1836. m. Pres. State
University of Oregon.

WILLIAM WOOLSEY JOHNSON   *Annapolis, Md.*
M.A. b. at Owego, N. Y., June 23, 1841. m. Prof. of
Mathematics at Kenyon College, Ohio. Corresponding
member of the British Ass'n for the Advancement of
Science. Author of treatises on Analytical Geometry,
Differential Calculus, and Integral Calculus.

ALBERT FRANCIS JUDD.   *Honolulu, H. I.*
LL.B. Harv., M.A., LL.D. b. at Honolulu, H. I., Jan. 7,
1838. m. Lawyer. Chief Justice of Supreme Court of
Hawaiian Islands.

THOMAS BURGIS KIRBY   *Washington, D. C.*
b. at New Haven, Conn., Feb. 28, 1842. m. Newspaper
editor. Major in Army in Civil War.

CORNELIUS LADD KITCHEL   *New Haven, Conn.*
M.A., B.D. b. at Plymouth Hollow, Conn., July 5, 1841.
m. Minister. Instructor at Yale.

FRANKLIN MACVEAGH   *Chicago, Ill.*
LL.B. Col. b. at West Chester, Pa., Nov. 22, 1837. m.
Wholesale grocery business.

RICHARD CARY MORSE   *New York City.*
M.A. b. at Greenport, N. J., Sept. 19, 1841. m. Active in Y. M. C. A. work.

THOMAS HUBBARD PITKIN   *Detroit, Mich.*
M.A. b. at Louisville, Ky., March 30, 1842. Teacher.

JOSEPH FITZ RANDOLPH   *Morristown, N. J.*
M.A. b. at New Brunswick, N. J., Dec. 4, 1843. m. Lawyer.

ALBERT BENJAMIN SHEARER   *Philadelphia, Pa.*
M.A. b. at Montgomery, Pa., Sept. 18, 1837. Lawyer.

GROSVENOR STARR
b. at New York City, Aug. 27, 1842. In Army in Civil War. d. 1862.

HENRY HAMLIN STEBBINS   *Rochester, N. Y.*
D.D. Hamilton. b. at New York City, June 3, 1839. m. Minister.

JOHN PHELPS TAYLOR   *Andover, Mass.*
M.A. b. at Andover, Mass., April 6, 1841. m. Minister. Theological Professor.

MATTHEW HUESTON THOMS
M.A., LL.B. Harv. and Col. · b. at Hamilton, O. Lawyer. d. 1890.

THOMAS GAIRDNER THURSTON
b. at Kailua, H. I., May 9, 1836. m. Minister. d. 1884.

ROGER SHERMAN TRACY   *New York City.*
M.D. P. and S. b. at Windsor, Vt., Dec. 9, 1841. Physician. Writer on hygienic subjects.

FREDERICK AUGUSTUS WARD   *Brooklyn, N. Y.*
LL.B. Col., M.A. b at Farmington, Conn., April 1, 1841. m. Lawyer.

BUCHANAN WINTHROP   *New York City.*
LL.B. Col., M.A. b. at New York City, Nov. 11, 1841. m. Lawyer. Member of Yale Corporation.

ROBERT GALBRAITH WOODS
b. at Salem, Ohio. Lawyer. Newspaper editor. d. 1873.

1863

GEORGE WILLIAM BAIRD   *Chicago, Ill.*
  b. at Milford, Conn., Dec. 13, 1839. m. Major in the Pay
  Department of the Army. In Army in Civil War.

GEORGE WALLACE BANKS   *Guilford, Conn.*
  b. at Greenfield Hill, Conn., July 11, 1839. m. Minister.

FREDERICK JONES BARNARD   *Worcester, Mass.*
  M.A., LL.B. Harv. b. at Worcester, Mass., Aug. 24, 1841.
  m. Lawyer. In Army in Civil War.

JACOB BERRY
  M.A. b. at Clarence, N. Y., Oct. 4, 1834. m. Teacher.
  d. 1881.

EGBERT BYRON BINGHAM
  b. at Scotland, Conn., Feb. 17, 1839. m. Minister. d.
  1891.

CHARLES CARROLL BLATCHLEY
  b. at North Madison, Conn., July 28, 1841. m. Real
  estate business. d. 1887.

ORLANDO FRANKLIN BUMP
  M.A. b. at Afton, N. Y., Feb. 28, 1841. m. Lawyer.
  Author of "The Law and Practice of Banking," "The
  Law of Patents, Trademarks and Copyright." d. 1884.

HORACE BUMSTEAD   *Atlanta, Ga.*
  M.A., D.D. U. C. N. Y. b. at Boston, Mass., Sept. 29,
  1841. m. President of Atlanta University.

GEORGE HAWKINS BUNDY   *Worcester, Mass.*
  M.A. b. at Springfield, Vt., Aug. 17, 1841. m. Soap
  business.

JOHN HASKELL BUTLER   *Boston, Mass.*
  b. at Middleton, Mass., Aug. 31, 1841. m. Lawyer.
  Member of the Executive Council of Mass. Pres. of
  Middlesex Club.

LEANDER TROWBRIDGE CHAMBERLAIN   *New York City.*
  D.D. U. of Vt. b. at West Brookfield, Mass., Sept. 26,
  1858. Minister. In Navy in Civil War.

EDWIN HENRY COOPER   *Henderson, Ill.*
  M.D. Rush. b. at Henderson, Ill., Jan. 3, 1843. Physician.

HENRY FARNAM DIMOCK *New York City.*
M.A. b. at South Coventry, Conn., March 28, 1842. m.
Lawyer.

WILLIAM BURR DUNNING
M.D. P. and S. b. at Peekskill, N. Y., Dec. 22, 1842. m.
Teacher. Physician. d. 1888.

BENJAMIN EGLIN *Lewinsville, Va.*
M.A., LL.B. Columbian U. b. at Ithaca, N. Y., April 28,
1838. m. In Treasury office at Washington.

THOMAS ALBERT EMERSON *Clinton, Conn.*
b. at South Reading, Mass., Dec. 27, 1840. m. Minister.
In Navy in Civil War.

HORACE WEBSTER FOWLER
LL.B. Col. b. at Elmira, N. Y., Oct. 31, 1842. Lawyer.
d. 1888.

CYRUS WEST FRANCIS *Brookfield Center, Conn.*
M.A., B.D. b. at Newington, Conn., June 17, 1838. m.
Minister. Theological Professor.

THOMAS HART FULLER *Washington, D. C.*
M.A. b. at Lisbon, Conn., Feb. 22, 1840. Teacher. In
P. O. Department at Washington.

JOSEPH FITCH GAYLORD *Barre, Mass.*
M.A. b. at Norfolk, Conn., Nov. 4, 1836. m. Minister.

EDWARD BRODIE GLASGOW *Worcester, Mass.*
M.A. b. at Philadelphia, Pa., March 9, 1843. Lawyer.

GEORGE SCOVILL HAMLIN *New York City.*
LL.B. Col. b. at Sharon, Conn., May 12, 1838. m.
Lawyer.

WILLABE HASKELL *New Haven, Conn.*
M.A., Ph.D. b. at Freeport, Me., Dec. 19, 1838. m. In
charge of Yale Reading Room.

THORNTON MILLS HINKLE *Cincinnati, O.*
LL.B. Col., M.A. b. at Cincinnati, O., Aug. 17, 1840. m.
Lawyer.

SAMUEL SHOREY HOLLINGSWORTH
M.A. b. at Cleveland, O., Nov. 11, 1842. m. Lawyer.
Prof. of Law at U. of P. d. 1894.

WILBUR IVES

M.A.　b. at Hamden, Conn., Jan. 3, 1843.　Paymaster in Navy in Civil War.　d. 1870.

JOSIAH JEWETT　　　　　　　　　　　　　　　　*Buffalo, N. Y.*

M.A.　b. at Buffalo, N. Y., Oct. 4, 1842.　m.　Stove business.

JOSEPH FREDERIC KERNOCHAN　　　　　　*New York City.*

LL.B. Col.　b. at New York City, Dec. 8, 1842.　m.　Lawyer.

HOWARD KINGSBURY

b. at New York City, Feb. 3, 1842.　m.　Minister.　d. 1878.

GEORGE EDWARD LOUNSBURY　　　　　*South Norwalk, Conn.*

b. at Ridgefield, Conn., Dec. 7, 1839.　Manufacturing business.

ROBERT GEORGE STEPHEN MCNEILLE　　　　*Pine Bluff, N. C.*

M.A., B.D.　b. at Philadelphia, Pa., April 1, 1841.　m. Lawyer.　Minister.

JOSEPH NAPHTHALY　　　　　　　　　　*San Francisco, Cal.*

M.A.　b. at Gostyn, Prussia.　m.　Lawyer.　Member of California Legislature.

ERASTUS NEW

M.A.　b. at Philmont, N. Y., Dec. 12, 1837.　m.　Lawyer. d. 1886.

DAVID BRAINERD PERRY　　　　　　　　　　*Crete, Neb.*

M.A., B.D.　b. at Worcester, Mass., Mar. 7, 1839.　m. President of Doane College.

HENRY SELDEN PRATT　　　　　　　　　*Springfield, Mass.*

M.A.　b. at Meriden, Conn., Jan. 9, 1841.　m.　Teacher.

WILLIAM CHURCHILL READE　　　　　　　　*Beverly, Mass.*

b. at. Hampden, Me., Nov. 1, 1835.　m.　Minister.

WALTER HEBERT SMYTH

b. at Guilford, Conn., May 11, 1843.　d. 1863.

WILLIAM GRAHAM SUMNER　　　　　　　*New Haven, Conn.*

LL.D. U. of Tenn.　b. at Paterson, N. J., Oct. 30, 1840. m.　Professor of Political and Social Science at Yale.

Author of "History of American Currency." "History of Protection in the United States," "Life of Andrew Jackson."

GEORGE KEYES TUFTS   *New Braintree, Mass.*
b. at New Braintree, Mass., Oct. 17, 1841. m. Manufacturing business. Member of Mass. Leg.

MOSES HUBBARD TUTTLE
b. at Sheffield, Mass., June 23, 1839. Cotton business. In Army in Civil War.

ALEXANDER HAMILTON WRIGHT
LL.B. Columbian U. b. at Lebanon, Conn., Sept. 1, 1838. Lawyer. d. 1896.

1864

CHARLES LARNED ATTERBURY   *New York City.*
b. at Detroit, Mich., Dec. 3, 1842. m. Lawyer.

WALTER WESLEY BATTERSHALL   *Albany, N. Y.*
M.A., D.D. Union. b. at Troy, N. Y., Jan. 8, 1840. m. Minister.

JOHN WICKLIFFE BEACH
M.A., B.D. b. at Wolcott, Conn., Jan. 5, 1843. m. Minister. Teacher. d. 1887.

CHARLES EDWARD BOOTH
b. at New York City, March 27, 1843. Business. d. 1870.

HENRY PAYNE BOYDEN   *Cincinnati, O.*
b. at Machias, Me., Feb. 12, 1842. m. Newspaper editor.

WILLIAM JESSUP CHANDLER   *South Orange, N. J.*
M.D. Col. b. at Montrose, Pa., July 11, 1842. m. Surgeon.

DANIEL LATHROP COIT
b. at Norwich, Conn., Nov. 22, 1843. In Army in Civil War. d. 1865.

SAMUEL CARTER DARLING   *Boston, Mass.*
LL.B. Albany, M.A. b. at St. Stephen's, N. B., Mar. 5, 1843. m. Lawyer. Member of Mass. Leg.

ORSON GREGORY DIBBLE   *Pompey, N. Y.*
M.A., M.D. U. C. N. Y. b. at Cortland, N. Y., Oct. 28,
1840. Physician.

TIMOTHY MILLER GRIFFING   *Riverhead, N. Y.*
LL.B. Albany, M.A. b. at Riverhead, N. Y., Nov. 22,
1842. m. Lawyer.

THOMAS HOOKER   *New York City.*
b. at Hartford, Conn., Oct. 22, 1844. m. Lawyer.

THEODORE WELD HOPKINS   *Rochester, N. Y.*
M.A., D.D. b. at Cincinnati, O., Jan. 5, 1841. Minister.
Theological Professor.

JAMES PHILLIPS HOYT   *Cheshire, Conn.*
M.A., B.D. b. at Coventry, N. Y., July 28, 1844. m.
Minister.

WALTER JUDSON   *New Haven, Conn.*
M.A., M.D. P. and S. b. at Bristol, Conn., May 1,
1840. m. Physician.

DAVID GILBERT LAPHAM   *Canandaigua, N. Y.*
M.A. b. at Manchester, N. Y., Jan. 17, 1839. m. Lawyer.

FRANCIS ENGLESBY LOOMIS   *care of Baring Bros., London, Eng.*
M.A., Ph.D. and Göttingen. b. at Hudson, O., July 26,
1842.

WILLIAM McAFEE
A.M. b. at Enniskillen, Ireland, May 18, 1844.   m.
Pres. of Claverack College. d. 1896.

CHARLES FRAZER McLEAN   *New York City.*
Ph.D., J. U. D. Berlin. b. at Utica, N. Y., Nov. 21, 1842.
m. Lawyer. President of Board of Police Commission-
ers of New York City 1890-1892. Judge of the Supreme
Court of New York.

GEORGE SPRING MERRIAM   *Springfield, Mass*
M.A. b. at Springfield, Mass., Jan. 13, 1843. m. Magazine editor. Letters. Author of " The Story of William
and Lucy Smith," " Noah Porter, a Memorial by Friends,"
" The Chief End of Man."

HORACE DANIEL PAINE
b. at Woonsocket, R. I., Oct. 24, 1841. Teacher. d. 1867.

4

WILLIAM HENRY PALMER
    M.D. P. and S.   b. at Stonington, Conn., Aug. 17, 1840.
    m. Physician. d. 1871.

ISAAC PLATT PUGSLEY   *Toledo, O.*
    M.A. b. at Goshen, N. Y., June 5, 1843. m. Lawyer.
    Judge of the Court of Common Pleas in Ohio. In Navy
    in Civil War.

CHARLES GREENE ROCKWOOD   *Princeton, N. J.*
    M.A. Bowdoin, Ph.D. b. at New York City, Jan. 11,
    1843. m. Professor of Mathematics at Princeton. Fel-
    low of American Ass'n for the Advancement of Science.

MURRAY COLEGATE SHOEMAKER
    LL.B. Col. b. at Tiffin, O., Sept. 18, 1844. m. Lawyer.
    d. 1885.

JOHN WILLIAM STERLING   *New York City.*
    M.A., LL.D., LL.B. Col. b. at Stratford, Conn., Nov. 12,
    1844. Lawyer.

CHARLES PHELPS TAFT   *Cincinnati, O.*
    M.A., LL.B. Col., J. U. D. Heidelberg. b. at Cincinnati,
    O., Dec. 21, 1843. m. Lawyer. Newspaper editor.
    Member of Congress.

JOHN WILLIAM TEAL
    M.A., D.D. Lafayette. b. at Rhinebeck, N. Y., April 14,
    1839. m. Minister. d. 1894.

JAMES HARVEY VAN GELDER   *Catskill, N. Y.*
    M.A., LL.B. Albany. b. at Catskill, N. Y., Nov. 4, 1838.
    m. Teacher. Lecturer. Hotel proprietor.

EDWIN FORCE WARREN   *Nebraska City, Neb.*
    M.A. b. at Jamestown, N. Y., Sept. 3, 1841. m. Lawyer.

CLARENCE LINCOLN WESTCOTT   *New York City.*
    b. at Wilton, Conn., June 17, 1843. m. Lawyer.

RALPH WHEELER   *New London, Conn.*
    b. at Stonington, Conn., May 14, 1843. m. Lawyer.
    Member of Conn. Leg. Mayor of New London. Judge
    of the Superior Court of Conn.

LEWIS FREDERICK WHITIN   *New York City.*
    M.A. b. at Whitinsville, Mass., Feb. 20, 1844. m. Busi-
    ness.

CHARLES MILLS WHITTELSEY   *Providence, R. I.*
  b. at Jaffna, Ceylon, July 15, 1842. m. Minister.

JOB WILLIAMS   *Hartford, Conn.*
  M.A., L.H.D. Nat. Deaf Mute Coll.   b. at Pomfret,
  Conn., March 1, 1842. m. Principal of American Asylum
  for the Deaf and Dumb.

MOSELEY HOOKER WILLIAMS   *Philadelphia, Pa.*
  M.A. b. at Farmington, Conn., Dec. 23, 1839. m. Minister. Periodical editor.

ORSON SUMMER WOOD   *Windsorville, Conn.*
  b. at Mansfield, Conn., Nov. 15, 1839. m. Farmer.
  Member of Conn. Legislature.

FRANCIS EBEN WOODRUFF   *Morristown, N. J.*
  b. at New York City, April 24, 1844. Custom Service of
  China.

1865

ELMER BRAGG ADAMS   *St. Louis, Mo.*
  b. at Pomfret, Vt., Oct. 27, 1842. m. Lawyer. Judge of
  the Circuit Court of Missouri.

JOHN FORSYTH ALLEN   *Pittsfield, Mass.*
  b. at Pittsfield, Mass., Aug. 26, 1841. m. Coal business.

SIMEON OLMSTED ALLEN   *West Springfield, Mass.*
  M.A., B.D. b. at Enfield, Conn., Dec. 23, 1837. m. Minister.

JOSIAH HOOKER BISSELL   *Chicago, Ill.*
  M.A. b. at Rochester, N. Y., June 1, 1845. Lawyer.

CHARLES EDWARD BLAKE   *San Francisco, Cal.*
  M.D. Pacific. b. at Holden, Me., Aug. 14, 1845. m. Physician.

CHARLES PINCKNEY BLANCHARD   *Brookfield, Mass.*
  M.A. b. at Richmond, Ind., Mar. 13, 1843. m. Minister.

JOHN EDWARD BROOKS   *New York City.*
  LL.B. Col. b. at Rye, N. Y., May 6, 1844. Lawyer.

TOLIVER FRANKLIN CASKEY   *Dresden, Ger.*
  b. at Fort Black, O., Aug. 29, 1838. m. Minister.

ADELBERT PUTNAM CHAPMAN   *New Haven, Conn.*
  b. at Ellington, Conn, Oct. 17, 1844.   m.   Minister.

HENRY CHURCHILL   *Herkimer, N. Y.*
  b. at Gloversville, N. Y., June 15, 1844.   m.   Paper business.   Banker.

HENRY PARK COLLIN   *Coldwater, Mich.*
  M.A.   b. at Benton, N. Y., July 26, 1843.   m.   Minister.

WILLIAMS TOMPKINS COMSTOCK   *New York City.*
  M.A.   b. at Reading, Conn., July 14, 1842.   m.   Publisher
  of books and magazines on architecture.

JOHN LEWIS EWELL   *Washington, D. C.*
  b. at Rowley, Mass., Sept. 4, 1840.   m.   Minister.   Theological Professor.

MARSHALL RICHARD GAINES   *Austin, Tex.*
  M.A., B.D.   b. at Granby, Conn., Nov. 15, 1839,   m.
  Minister.   Teacher.   Pres. of Tillotson College.

JAMES GLYNN GREGORY   *Norwalk, Conn.*
  M.D. P. and S.   b. at Norwalk, Conn., May 12, 1843.   m.
  Physician.   Member of Conn. Legislature.

MILES GOODYEAR HYDE   *New York City.*
  M.D. Geneva, M.A.   b. at Cortland, N. Y., June 12, 1841.
  m.   Physician.   Letters.

JOSEPH HENRY ISHAM
  B.D.   b. at Auburn, N. Y., March 2, 1842.   Minister.   d.
  1884.

ROBERT PORTER KEEP   *Norwich, Conn.*
  Ph.D., M.A.   b. at Farmington, Conn., April 26, 1844.
  m.   Principal of Norwich Free Academy.   Author of
  "Homeric Dictionary," "Stories from Herodotus."

CHARLES HENRY LEONARD   *Providence, R. I.*
  M.D. P. and S., M.A.   b. at Madison, Ind., Dec. 29, 1841.
  m.   Physician.

PAYSON MERRILL   *New York City.*
  LL.B. Col.   b. at Stratham, N. H., Dec. 7, 1842.   m.
  Lawyer.

WILLIS LONG REEVES   *Elkton, Ky.*
  b. at Elkton, Ky., Sept. 6, 1841. m. Lawyer. Circuit
Judge in Kentucky. Member of the Kentucky Leg.

BENJAMIN CLAPP RIGGS
  M.D. P. and S. b. at St. Louis, Mo., Feb. 16, 1845. m.
Physician. d. 1883.

CHARLES HENRY SMITH   *New Haven, Conn.*
  LL.D. Bowdoin. b. at Beirut, Syria, May 14, 1842. m.
Professor of History at Yale.

HENRY ALBERT STIMSON   *St. Louis, Mo.*
  D.D., M.A. · b. at New York City, Sept. 28, 1842. m.
Minister.

WILLIAM STOCKING   *Detroit, Mich.*
  M.A. b. at Waterbury, Conn., Dec. 11, 1840. m. Newspaper editor.

LOUIS STOSKOPF
  M.D. P. and S., M.A. b. at Freeport, Ill., Nov. 14, 1842.
m. Physician. d. 1865.

CORYDON GILES STOWELL   *Chicago, Ill.*
  M.A. b. at Tully, N. Y., July 27, 1839. m. Principal of
Newberry School, Chicago.

HENRY ELLSWORTH TAINTOR   *Hartford, Conn.*
  b. at Hampton, Conn., Aug. 29, 1844. m. Lawyer.

GOUVERNEUR MORRIS THOMPSON   *New York City.*
  LL.B. Albany. b. at Bridgeport, Conn., Feb. 4, 1844.
Lawyer.

HENRY WATERMAN WARREN   *Holden, Mass.*
  b. at Auburn, Mass., March 18, 1838. m. Leather business. Mem. of Mass. Leg.

EDWIN HORACE WILSON   *Cambridge, Mass.*
  M.A. b. at Westmoreland, N. Y., Oct. 4, 1839. m. Principal of college preparatory school.

JOHN BRANDEGEE WOOD   *Nutley, N. J.*
  LL.B. Col. b. at Morristown, N. J., June 25, 1844. m.
Lawyer. Letters.

1866

CHARLES HEMMENWAY ADAMS   *Hartford, Conn.*
b. at Fairfield, Conn., Sept. 26, 1846. Newspaper editor.

WILLIAM HENRY BENNETT   *Minneapolis, Minn.*
LL.B. Albany. b. at Scotland, Conn., June 24, 1843. m.
Lawyer.

MARCELLUS BOWEN   *Constantinople, Turkey.*
b. at Marion, O., April 6, 1846. Minister. Teacher. Agent
for the Levant of the American Bible Society.

WILLIAM GEORGE BUSSEY   *New York City.*
b. at Utica, N. Y., Feb. 17, 1846. m. Lawyer.

FRANK SMITH CHAPIN   *Tulare, Cal.*
b. at East Bloomfield, N. Y., April 21, 1843. m. Fruit
business. Newspaper writer. Lecturer.

CASSIUS MARCELLUS CLAY   *Paris, Ky.*
b. at Paris, Ky., Mar. 26, 1846. m. Farmer. Member of
Kentucky Leg.

EDMUND COFFIN   *New York City.*
LL.B. Col. b. at New York City, Nov. 8, 1844. m.
Lawyer.

HAMILTON COLE
b. at Claverack, N. Y., May 4, 1845. Lawyer. d. 1889.

MAURICE DWIGHT COLLIER   *New York City.*
M.A., LL.B. Wash. U. b. at St. Louis, Mo., May 6, 1846.
m. Lawyer.

CHARLES AVERY COLLIN   *New York City.*
M.A. b. at Benton, N. Y., May 18, 1846. m. Lawyer.

JAMES LEWIS COWLES   *Farmington, Conn.*
LL.B. b. at Farmington, Conn., Sept. 14, 1843. m.
Manufacturing business. Lawyer.

JOHN KENNEDY CREEVEY   *Brooklyn, N. Y.*
b. at Cross Hill, Ireland, Aug. 13, 1841. m. Lawyer.

JAMES CLOYD DOTY. b. at Mifflintown, Pa., June 21, 1844.
m. Lawyer. d. 1895.

HARRISON DOWNES   *New York City.*
LL.B. Col. b. at Northville, N. Y., Sept. 1, 1843. Lawyer.

HENRY WARD FOOTE
    M.A. b. at Cincinnati, O., Aug. 5, 1844. Law student.
    d. 1875.

JAMES TAYLOR GRAVES   *Chicago, Ill.*
    b. at Townsend, Vt., Feb. 2, 1843. m. Minister.

ALBERT FRANCIS HALE   *Ridgefield, Ill.*
    M.A., B.D. b. at Springfield, Mass., Oct. 2, 1844. m.
    Minister.

LORENZO HALL   *Albany, N. Y.*
    M.D. Albany. b. at Albany, N. Y., Sept. 7, 1844. m.
    Physician.

LOVELL HALL   *Middletown, Conn.*
    M.A., LL.B. Col. b. at East Hampton, Conn., May 12,
    1844. Lawyer.

FREDERICK NEWTON JUDSON   *St. Louis, Mo.*
    M.A., LL.B. Wash. U. b. at St. Mary's, Ga., Oct. 7,
    1845. m. Lawyer.

†HENRY BURNHAM MEAD   *Scotland, Conn.*
    M.A., B.D. b. at Littleton, N. H., Jan. 27, 1839. m.
    Minister.

GEORGE SHIPMAN PAYSON   *New York City.*
    b. at Harpersfield, N. Y., Sept. 11, 1845. m. Minister.

ISAAC PIERSON   *West Medford, Mass.*
    b. at Orange, N. J., Aug. 11, 1843. m. Missionary in
    China.

DARIUS PARMALEE SACKETT   *Brooklyn, N. Y.*
    M.A. b. at Tallmadge, O., Sept. 22, 1842. m. Principal
    of boys' school.

SAMUEL BENEDICT ST. JOHN   *Hartford, Conn.*
    M.D. P. and S. b. at Hudson, O., July 24, 1845. m.
    Specialist of the eye and ear.

HENRY THOMPSON SLOANE   *New York City.*
    b. at New York City, Dec. 1, 1845. m. Carpet business.

CHARLES McLELLAN SOUTHGATE   *Auburndale, Mass.*
    b. at Monroe, Mich., Nov. 18, 1845. m. Minister.

SIEGWART SPIER   *New Haven, Conn.*
    b. in Germany. m. Lawyer.

WILLIAM EGBERT WHEELER *Portville, N. Y.*
M.A. b. at Portville, N. Y., Nov. 21, 1844. m. Lumber and oil business.

GEORGE EDWARD WHITE *Stamford, Conn.*
M.A. b. at New Haven, Conn., Mar. 17, 1845. m. Manufacturing business.

HENRY OTIS WHITNEY
b. at Williston, Vt., Dec. 6, 1840. Minister. d. 1870.

1867

ARTHUR HERMAN ADAMS
M.D. b. at Florence, O., Nov. 24, 1847. m. Medical missionary. d. 1879.

FRANK LEE BALDWIN *Massillon, O.*
M.A. b. at Massillon, O., July 19, 1846. Lawyer.

GEORGE COTTON BRAINERD *New York City.*
M.A., LL.B. Harv. b. St. Albans, Vt., Nov. 23, 1845. Lawyer.

LEONARD TREAT BROWN
b. at Lebanon, Conn., Dec. 26, 1846. Teacher. d. 1880.

WALLACE BRUCE *Brooklyn, N. Y.*
b. at Hillsdale, N. Y., Nov. 10, 1844. m. Lecturer.

DAVID JAMES BURRELL *New York City.*
D.D. elsewhere. b. at Mt. Pleasant, Pa., Aug. 1, 1841. m. Minister.

CHARLES KINSEY CANNON *Hoboken, N. J.*
M.A., LL.B. Col. b. at Bordentown, N. J., Nov. 12, 1846. Lawyer.

JOHN HENRY CHAPMAN *Sioux Falls, S. D.*
M.A. b. at Nashua, N. H., Sept. 14, 1844. m. Farmer.

CHARLES GOODRICH COE *New York City.*
LL.B. Col. b. at Ridgefield, Conn., Aug. 18, 1846. Lawyer.

CHARLES TERRY COLLINS
b. at Hartford, Conn., Oct. 14, 1845. m. Minister. d. 1883.

THEODORE LANSING DAY
M.A., B.D. b. at Boston, Mass., Sept. 18, 1845. m. Minister. d. 1885.

MORTON DEXTER   *Boston, Mass.*
M.A. b. at Manchester, N. H., July 12, 1846. Literary editor of the Congregationalist.

ALBERT ELIJAH DUNNING   *Boston, Mass.*
D.D. Beloit. b. at Brookfield, Conn., Jan. 5, 1844. m. Editor of the Congregationalist.

HENRY TURNER EDDY   *Cincinnati, O.*
Ph.B. and M.A., C.E. and Ph.D. Cor. b. at Stoughton, Mass., June 9, 1844. m. Prof. of Mathematics at Cornell and Princeton, Prof. of Mech. and Engin. at U. of Minnesota. Vice-President American Ass'n for the Advancement of Science. Author of "Analytic Geometry," "Thermodynamics."

JAMES GREELEY FLANDERS   *Milwaukee, Wis.*
LL.B. Col. b. at New London, N. H., Dec. 13, 1844. m. Lawyer. Member of the Wisconsin Leg.

THOMAS GREENWOOD
LL.B. Col. b. at Providence, R. I., Nov. 27, 1842. Lawyer. U. S. Ass't District Attorney. d. 1894.

WILDER BENNETT HARDING   *Salem, N. Y.*
M.A. b. at Putney, Vt., Feb. 6, 1841. m. Principal of the Genesee Valley Seminary.

SAMUEL KEELER   *New York City.*
b. at Wilton, Conn., Nov. 22, 1845. Lawyer.

LUTHER HART KITCHEL   *Corfu, N. Y.*
M.D. P. and S. b. at Plymouth Hollow, Conn., Nov. 6, 1845. m. Physician.

JAMES FISKE MERRIAM   *Springfield, Mass.*
b. at Springfield, Mass., May 2, 1845. m. Minister.

ALFRED EUGENE NOLEN   *Fitchburg, Mass.*
M.A. b. at Leicester, Mass., Dec. 25, 1845. Teacher.

JOHN WARREN PARTRIDGE
b. at Princeton, Mass., Sept. 24, 1844. m. Minister. d. 1889.

GEORGE HENRY PERKINS   *Burlington, Vt.*
Ph.D. b. at East Cambridge, Mass., Sept. 25, 1844. m.
Professor of Natural History in U. of Vermont.

PETER BRYNBERG PORTER   *New York City.*
M.D. U. of P.   b. at Wilmington, Del., Jan. 17, 1845.
Physician.

GEORGE PRESTON SHELDON   *New York City.*
LL.B. Col. b. at New York City, Jan. 17, 1847. m.
Lawyer. Insurance business.

HENRY CLAY SHELDON   *Boston, Mass.*
M.A., S.T.B. Boston U.   b. at Martinsburg, N. Y., Mar.
12, 1845. m. Prof. of Theology at Boston U. Author
of "The History of Christian Doctrine."

BENJAMIN SMITH   *Newtown, Pa.*
M.A. b. at Solebury, Pa., Aug. 1, 1840. m. Professor
of Rhetoric and Philosophy at Swarthmore College.

JAMES MAGOFFIN SPENCER   *Munich, Germany.*
M.A., LL.B. Albany. b. at Brooklyn, N. Y., April 9,
1839. m. Professor in Nat. Deaf and Dumb College at
Washington.

PETER RAWSON TAFT
M.A. b. at Cincinnati, O., May 10, 1846. m. d. 1889.

EDGAR ABEL TURRELL   *New York City.*
M.A., LL.B. Col. b. at Montrose, Pa., Aug. 5, 1845.
Lawyer.

BOYD VINCENT   *Cincinnati, O.*
M.A., D.D. Trinity.   b. at Erie, Pa., May 18, 1845. Asst.
Bishop of Southern Ohio.

CHARLES SWAN WALKER   *Amherst, Mass.*
M.A. and B.D., Ph.D. Amherst. b. in Cincinnati, O., Oct.
7, 1846. m. Minister.

ALBERT WARREN   *Lake Benton, Minn.*
B.D. b. at Leicester, Mass., Feb. 14, 1844. m. Teacher.
Minister.

RICHARD WILLIAM WOODWARD   *Franklin, Conn.*
b. at Franklin, Conn., Dec. 8, 1846. Chemist. Coal
business.

1868

ISBON THADDEUS BECKWITH   *Hartford, Conn.*
Ph.D. b. at Old Lyme, Conn., Oct. 18, 1843. Prof. of
Greek at Trinity,

ALGERNON SIDNEY BIDDLE
M.A. b. at Philadelphia, Pa., Oct. 11, 1847. m. Lawyer.
Prof. of Law at U. of P. d. 1891.

CHAUNCEY BUNCE BREWSTER   *Hartford, Conn.*
M.A. b. at Windham, Conn., Sept. 5, 1848. m. Minister.
Bishop Coadjutor of Conn.

TIMOTHY PITKIN CHAPMAN
LL.B. Col. b. at Bridgeport, Conn., June 24, 1848. m.
Lawyer. d. 1875.

JAMES COFFIN   *Ross, Cal.*
b. at New York City, Oct. 13, 1847. m. Banker. Broker.

SILAS AUGUSTUS DAVENPORT   *Okeson, Pa.*
M.D. P. and S. b. at Brooklyn, N. Y., June 27, 1846. m.
Minister.

JOHN KINNE HYDE DEFOREST   *Sendai, Japan.*
B.D., D.D. b. at Westbrook, Conn., June 20, 1845. m.
Missionary. Author of " Education in Japan," " Popular
Aspects of Buddhism," " The Basis of Society."

CORNELIUS DUBOIS   *New York City.*
M.A. b. at Poughkeepsie, N. Y., July 7, 1845. Lawyer.

GEORGE EASTBURN   *Philadelphia, Pa.*
M.A., Ph.D. Princeton. b. at Solebury, Pa., Sept. 25,
1838. m. Principal of Eastburn Academy.

CHARLES HENRY FARNAM   *New York City.*
M.A., LL.B. Col. b. at New Haven, Conn., Sept. 12, 1846.
m. Lawyer. Ass't in Archæology at Yale.

JOSEPH WARREN GREENE   *Brooklyn, N. Y.*
LL.B. Col. b. at Brooklyn, N. Y., Nov. 2, 1846. m.
Lawyer.

OSCAR HARGER
M.A. b. at Oxford, Conn., Jan. 12, 1843. m. Ass't in

Paleontology at Yale. Author of "Report on the Marine Isopoda of New England." d. 1887.

FRANCIS HUNT HOLMES
b. at Williamsburg, Mass., Jan. 12, 1839. Teacher. Newspaper editor. d. about 1880.

ROBERT ALLEN HUME *Ahmednagar, W. India.*
M.A., D.D. b. at Bombay, India, March 18, 1847. m. Missionary in India.

EDWARD ALEXANDER LAWRENCE
M.A., D.D. Beloit. b. at Marblehead, Mass., Jan. 16, 1847. Minister. d. 1893.

GEORGE HENRY LEWIS *Des Moines, Iowa.*
M.A. and Iowa. b. at New Britain, Conn., Sept. 6, 1842. m. Real estate business. In Army in Civil War.

JOHN LEWIS *Oak Park, Ill.*
b. at Sheffield, Conn., June 22, 1842. m. Lawyer. In Army in Civil War. Author of "A Treatise on the Law of Eminent Domain in the United States."

EDWARD SPENCER MEAD
M.A. b. at Brooklyn, N. Y., Jan. 10, 1847. m. Publishing business. d. 1894.

ELISHA WRIGHT MILLER *Eaton Rapids, Mich.*
B.D. b. at Williston, Vt., Oct. 29, 1845. m. Minister.

GEORGE ALBERT NEWELL *Medina, N. Y.*
M.A. b. at Medina, N. Y., Jan. 11, 1846. m. Banking business.

SAMUEL PARRY *Pluckamin, N. J.*
M.A. b. at Lambertville, N. J., March 29, 1845. m. Minister.

HORACE PHILLIPS *Seattle, Wash.*
b. at Dayton, O., April 9, 1847. m. Railroad business.

THOMAS WILSON PIERCE *West Chester, Pa.*
M.A. b. at Birmingham, Pa., Aug. 3, 1845. m. Lawyer.

THOMAS HAMLIN ROBBINS *Arlington, Kansas.*
M.A. b. at Rocky Hill, Conn., Nov. 4, 1841. Civil engineer.

JULIUS WILLIAM RUSSELL   *Burlington, Vt.*
   b. at Moira, N. Y., Sept. 1, 1846. m. Lawyer.

FRANCIS EUGENE SEAGRAVE   *Toledo, Ohio.*
   b. at Bellingham, Mass., Nov. 5, 1843. m. Lawyer.

JAMES KINGSLEY THACHER
   M.D. b, at New Haven, Conn., Oct. 19, 1847. m. Prof.
   of Physiology at Yale Medical School. d. 1891.

ANSON PHELPS TINKER
   b. at Old Lyme, Conn., Oct. 15, 1884. m. Minister. d.
   1886.

SAMUEL TWEEDY   *Danbury, Conn.*
   b. at Danbury, Conn., April 21, 1846. m. Lawyer.

JOHN LEONARD VARICK   *New York City.*
   b. at Poughkeepsie, N. Y., Dec. 1, 1846. m. Hardware
   business.

SAMUEL WATSON   *Nashville, Tenn.*
   LL.B. Harv. b. at Sycamore Mills, Tenn., July 11, 1846.
   Lawyer. Member of the Tenn. Leg.

JOHN HOWARD WEBSTER   *Cleveland, O.*
   M.A. b. at Portsmouth, N. H., Nov. 8, 1846. m. Lawyer.

THOMAS FENNER WENTWORTH   *New York City.*
   b. at South Berwick, Me., Sept. 25, 1845. m. Lawyer.

JOHN HOWARD WILSON   *New York City.*
   M.A. b. at Natick, Mass., March 9, 1847. m. Lawyer.

WILLIAM CURTIS WOOD
   M.A. b. at Mahableshwar, India, April 20, 1849. Tutor
   at Yale. d. 1875.

HENRY COLLINS WOODRUFF   *Black Rock, Conn.*
   b. at Brooklyn, N. Y., Feb. 16, 1845. m. Minister.

HENRY PARKS WRIGHT   *New Haven, Conn.*
   M.A., Ph.D. b. at Winchester, N. H., Nov. 30, 1839. m.
   Dean of Yale College. Prof. in Latin at Yale.

1869

HENRY CLAY BANNARD   *Chicago, Ill.*
    b. at New York City, Dec. 21, 1844. m. Lawyer.

CHARLES WILLIAM BARDEEN   *Syracuse, N. Y.*
    b. at Groton, Mass., Aug. 28, 1847. m. Managing editor
    of the "School Bulletin."

ALFRED BARTOW   *Chadron, Neb.*
    b. at Leroy, N. Y., Sept. 20, 1846. m. Lawyer. Mem-
    ber of Nebraska Leg.

HENRY AUGUSTIN BEERS   *New Haven, Conn.*
    M.A. b. at Buffalo, N. Y., July 2, 1847. m. Professor
    of English at Yale. Author of "The Thankless Muse,"
    "From Chaucer to Tennyson," "A Suburban Pastoral
    and Other Tales," "Ways of Yale."

SYLVESTER FORISTALL BUCKLIN
    b. at Marlboro, Mass., March 29, 1847. m. Farmer. d.
    1893.

FRANK RUSSELL CHILDS   *Hartford, Conn.*
    M.A. b. at E. Hartford, Conn., April 19, 1849. m.
    Teacher.

LEWIS ELLIOT CONDICT
    b. at Newark, N. J., Jan. 16, 1848. Lawyer. d. 1881.

EDWARD GUSTIN COY   *Lakeville, Conn.*
    M.A. b. at Ithaca, N. Y., Aug. 23, 1844. m. Teacher.
    Author of "Greek for Beginners," "First Greek Reader."

JOHN ELIASON
    M.D. Jefferson. b. at Chestertown, Md., July 29, 1848.
    Teacher. Medical student. d. 1873.

JOHN COWLES GRANT   *Chicago, Ill.*
    M.A. b. at Avon, Conn., April 21, 1848. m. Teacher.

CHARLES EDWARD GROSS   *Hartford, Conn.*
    M.A. b. at Hartford, Conn., Aug. 18, 1847. m. Lawyer.
    Pres. Hartford Board of Trade.

FREDERICK SMITH HAYDEN   *Jacksonville, Ill.*
    B.D., D.D. U. of Ill. b. at Rochester, N. Y., Aug. 23,
    1846. m. Minister.

EDWARD HEATON
 b. at Cincinnati, O., Sept. 29, 1842. m. Lawyer. In
 Army in Civil War. d. 1884.

EDWIN HEDGES
 b. at Sag Harbor, N. Y., Feb. 12, 1847. m. Lawyer. d.
 1881.

JOHN TEN BROECK HILLHOUSE   *New York City.*
 M.D. Col. b. at New York City, Oct. 24, 1848. m. Civil
 engineer.

THOMAS HOOKER   *New Haven, Conn.*
 M.A. b. at Macon, Ga., Sept. 3, 1849. m. Member of
 Board of Education of New Haven.

CHARLES AURELIUS HULL   *New York City.*
 b. at Brooklyn, N. Y., May 26, 1848. m. Insurance
 business.

ELY ISRAEL HUTCHINSON   *San Francisco, Cal.*
 b. at Kenosha, Wis., Aug. 22, 1847. m. Lawyer. Fruit
 grower.

JOHN BEACH ISHAM
 M.A., M.D. Bellevue. b. at New York City, March 28,
 1847. m. Physician. d. 1894.

JAMES JOY   *Detroit, Mich.*
 b. at Detroit, Mich., Nov. 14, 1847. m. Railroad business.

GARDINER LATHROP   *Kansas City, Mo.*
 M.A., LL.B. Harv. b. at Waukesha, Wis., Feb. 16, 1850.
 m. Lawyer.

HENRY LEAR   *Doylestown, Pa.*
 M.A. b. at Doylestown, Pa., Mar. 21, 1848. m. Lawyer.

ADRIAN VAN SINDEREN LINDSLEY   *Nashville, Tenn.*
 b. at Nashville, Tenn., Oct. 11, 1847. m. Real estate
 business.

DAVID MANNING   *Worcester, Mass.*
 b, at Paxton, Mass., Aug. 29, 1846. m. Lawyer.

HENRY CLAY MISSIMER   *Erie, Pa.*
 M.A. b. at Pottstown, Pa. m. Principal of Erie High
 School.

JOHN OLENDORF   *Jersey City, N. J.*
M.A. b. at Albany, N. Y., June 14, 1848. Lawyer.

BERNADOTTE PERRIN   *New Haven, Conn.*
Ph.D., LL.D. Western Reserve. b. at Goshen, Conn.,
Sept. 15, 1847. m. Professor of Greek at Yale. Editor
"Caesar's Gallic Wars," "Homer's Odyssey."

MOSES STUART PHELPS
Ph.D. b. at Andover, Mass., March 6, 1849. Professor of
Philosophy at Smith. d. 1883.

MITCHELL DAVISON RHAME   *Minneapolis, Minn.*
b. at East Rockaway, N. Y., Oct. 12, 1846. m. Railroad
engineer.

RUFUS BYAM RICHARDSON   *Athens, Greece.*
Ph.D., B.D. b. at Westford, Mass., April 18, 1845. m.
Teacher.

AUSTIN SCOTT   *New Brunswick, Conn.*
M.A., Ph.D. Leipzig, LL.D. Princeton. b. at Maumee
City, O., Aug. 10, 1848. m. President of Rutgers Col-
lege.

ARTHUR SHIRLEY   *Lyme, Conn.*
M.A., B.D. b. at Portland, Me., Nov. 19, 1845. m. Minister.

HENRY TAYLOR TERRY   *Hongo, Japan.*
b. at Hartford, Conn., Sept. 19, 1847. Lawyer. Professor
at University of Tokio. Author of "Leading Principles
of Anglo-American Law."

AARON SMITH THOMAS   *New York City.*
b. at Wickford, R. I., March 26, 1847. m. Shoe business.

CHARLES THEODORE WEITZEL
M.A. b. in Germany, May 12, 1847. m. Minister. d.
1896.

THEODORE FRELINGHUYSEN WELCH   *Buffalo, N. Y.*
b. at Gowanda, N. Y., Dec. 19, 1846. Teacher. Lawyer.

EDWARD PAYSON WILDER   .
LL.B. Col. b. in India. m. Lawyer. d. 1890.

FRANCKE SHERMAN WILLIAMS
M.A., LL.B. Col. b. at Newburyport, Mass., April 20, 1847. m. In Patent Office at Washington. d. 1882.

WILLIAM HUNTER WORKMAN   *Dresden, Ger.*
M.A., M.D. Harv. b. at Worcester, Mass., Feb. 16, 1847. m. Physician.

1870

JOHN WALLINGFORD ANDREWS
LL.B. Col. b. at Columbus, O., May 4, 1849. m. Lawyer. d. 1880.

WALTER ROGERS BEACH   *New York City.*
M.A. LL.B. Col. b. at Milford, Conn., Sept. 1, 1847. Lawyer.

GEORGE LUCIUS BEARDSLEY   *Bridgeport, Conn.*
M.A., M.D. b. at Milford, Conn., May 12, 1848. m. Physician.

WILLIAM JAMES BETTS   *Stamford, Conn.*
M.A. b. at Stamford, Conn., May 19, 1847. m. Principal of Betts Academy, Stamford, Conn.

WALTER BUCK   *Andover, Mass.*
b. at Boston, Mass., Sept. 24, 1847. m. Mortgage and real estate business.

NORMAN WHITE CARY   *Grosse Pointe, Mich.*
M.A. b. at New York City, Oct. 29, 1849. Minister.

JOHN SCUDDER CHANDLER   *Pasumalai, Southern India.*
M.A., B.D. b. at Madura, South India, April 12, 1849. m. Missionary.

GEORGE CHASE   *New York City.*
LL.B. Col. b. at Portland, Me., Dec. 29, 1849. m. Prof. at Columbia and at New York Law School.

ORLANDO COPE
b. at Mahoning Co., O., March 10, 1843. Civil engineer. d. 1871.

JOTHAM HENRY CUMMINGS   *Kerkhoven, Minn.*
b. at Worcester, Mass., April 1, 1847. m. Farmer.

5

EDWARD SALISBURY DANA　　　　　　　*New Haven, Conn.*
M.A., Ph.D.　b. at New Haven, Conn., Nov. 16, 1849.　m.
Prof. of Physics at Yale.　Curator of mineralogical cabi-
net in Peabody Museum in New Haven.　Corresponding
member of the K. K. Geologische Reichanstalt at Vienna.

ROBERT WEEKS DE FOREST　　　　　　　*New York City.*
M.A., LL.B. Col.　b. at New York City, April 25, 1848.
m.　Gen. Att'y for Central R. R. of N. J.　Sec'y of Yale
Association in New York City.

EDWARD SACKETT HUME　　　　　　*Byculla, Bombay, India.*
M.A.　b. at Bombay, India, June 4, 1848.　m.　Missionary.

FRANK FANNING JEWETT　　　　　　　　　　*Oberlin, O.*
M.A.　b. at Newton Corners, Mass., Jan. 8, 1844.　m.
Prof. of Chemistry and Mineralogy at, and Dean of,
Oberlin College.

CASSIUS WILLIAM KELLY　　　　　　　*West Superior, Wis.*
Ph.B.　b. at Pleasantville, Pa., May 10, 1848.　m.　Civil
engineer.

DWIGHT WHITNEY LEARNED　　　　　　　*Kyota, Japan.*
Ph.D.　b. at Canterbury, Conn., Oct. 12, 1848.　m.　Missionary and Prof. in Doshisha College, Kyoto, Japan.

PHILIP LINDSLEY　　　　　　　　　　*New York City.*
b. at Nashville, Tenn., Feb. 2., 1850.　Night editor " New
York Times."

WALTER SETH LOGAN　　　　　　　　*New York City.*
b. at Washington, Conn., April 15, 1847.　m.　Lawyer.

JAMES GORE KING McCLURE　　　　　　*Lake Forest, Ill.*
D.D. Lake Forest.　b. at Albany, N. Y., Nov. 24, 1848.
m.　Minister.　Pres. of Lake Forest University.

SAMUEL ST. JOHN McCUTCHEN　　　　　*Plainfield, N. J.*
LL.B.　b. at Williamsburg, N. Y., Jan. 14, 1849.　m.
Lawyer.

GEORGE DICKSON METCALF　　　　　　　*Berkeley, Cal.*
b. at Central, Ill., 1847.　m.　Lawyer.　　　　　·

SAMUEL ROSEBURGH MORROW　　　　　　*Albany, N. Y.*
M.A., M.D. P. and S. and Albany.　b. at Albany, N. Y.,
May 16, 1849.　m.　Physician.　Prof. Anat. and Orthoped.
Surg. at Albany Med. Coll.

JOHN HOYT PERRY   *Southport, Conn.*
   M.A., LL.B. Col. b. at Southport, Conn., July 26, 1848.
   m. Lawyer.

SANDS FISH RANDALL   *Brooklyn, N. Y.*
   LL.B. Col. b. at Mystic Bridge, Conn., May 18, 1846.
   Lawyer.

HENRY AUGUSTUS RILEY
   LL.B. Col. b. at Montrose, Pa., Dec. 20, 1848. m. Lawyer. d. 1892.

JOHN ALEXANDER ROSS   *Kansas City, Mo.*
   b. at Greenup, Ky., Jan. 27, 1850. m. Lawyer.

LAURISTON LIVINGSTON SCAIFE   *Boston, Mass.*
   M.A. b. at Pittsburgh, Pa., May 23, 1850. m. Lawyer.

CHARLES EDWARD SHEPARD   *Seattle, Wash.*
   b. at Dansville, N. Y., March 14, 1848. m. Lawyer.

RANDALL SPAULDING   *Montclair, N. J.*
   b. at Townsend, Mass., Feb. 3, 1845. m. Supt. of Public
   Schools.

EDWARD RUSSELL STEARNS   *Cincinnati, O.*
   M.A. b. at Cincinnati, O., Jan. 10, 1847. m. Manufacturing business.

CHARLES HALL STRONG   *Savannah, Ga.*
   M.A. b. at New Orleans, La., Dec. 29, 1850. m. Minister.

THOMAS JOSEPH TILNEY
   LL.B. Col. b. at Paris, Canada, Feb. 28, 1845. m. Manufacturing business. d. 1893.

MORRIS FRANK TYLER   *New Haven, Conn.*
   LL.B., M.A. b. at New Haven, Conn., Aug. 12, 1848. m.
   Lawyer. Prof. of Jurisprudence at Yale.

ARTHUR HENRY WARREN   *Leicester, Mass.*
   b. at Leicester, Mass., Aug. 26, 1846. m.

WILLIAM HENRY WELCH   *Baltimore, Md.*
   M.D. N. Y. Med. Coll. b. at Norfolk, Conn., April 3,
   1850. Prof. of Pathology at Johns Hopkins.

EDWARD SPENCER WHITE   *Hartford, Conn.*
   b. at Granby, Mass., March 12, 1848. m. Lawyer.

1871

ROBERT WODROW ARCHBALD *Scranton, Pa.*
b. at Carbondale, Pa., Sept. 10, 1848. m. Lawyer. Dist. Judge in Pa.

FREDERICK LAWTON AUCHINCLOSS
M.A. b. at New York City, Feb. 26, 1851. Dry goods business. d. 1878.

ALBERT PORTER BRADSTREET *Thomaston, Conn.*
LL.B. Col. b. at Thomaston, Conn., June 9, 1846. m. Lawyer.

JOSEPH ARTHUR BURR *Brooklyn, N. Y.*
LL.B. Col. b. at Williamsburg, N. Y., Sept. 11, 1850. m. Lawyer.

FREDERICK SIDNEY CHASE *Lafayette, Ind.*
LL.B. Col. b. at Lafayette, Ind., Dec. 31, 1849. m. Lawyer.

CHARLES HOPKINS CLARK. *Hartford, Conn.*
M.A. b. at Hartford, Conn., April 1, 1848. m. Editor "Hartford Courant."

CORNELIUS ELTING CUDDEBACK *Port Jervis, N. Y.*
LL.B. Col. b. at Port Jervis, N. Y., March 10, 1849. m. Lawyer.

CHARLES BENJAMIN DUDLEY *Altoona, Pa.*
Ph.D. b. at Oxford, N. Y., July 14, 1842. Chemist of Penn. R. R.

LUTHER FULLER *Washington, D. C.*
M.A. b. at Scotland, Conn., June 22, 1847. U. S. Patent Office.

EDWARD GRAY *San Francisco, Cal.*
M.D. P. and S. b. at Benicia, Cal., Nov. 17, 1849. m. Physician.

EDWARD BUCKINGHAM GUTHRIE *Buffalo, N. Y.*
b. at Putnam, O., July 25, 1849. m. Civil Engineer.

CHARLES HEZEKIAH HAMLIN *Easthampton, Mass.*
b. at Plainville, Conn., Jan. 11, 1850. m. Minister.

· CHARLES DANIEL HINE   *New Britain, Conn.*
    LL.B. U. of Iowa. b. at Fair Haven, Vt., Feb. 26, 1845.
    m. Teacher. Author of pamphlet "History of England
    Before the Conquest."

ALBERT EGBERT JANVIER   *Independence, Cal.*
    Miner.

FRANCIS SMITH JOHNSON   *Little Rock, Ark.*
    b. at Little Rock, Ark., Sept. 5, 1847. m. Att'y Mo.
    Pacific R. R.

HERBERT EVELYN KINNEY   *New York City.*
    LL.B. Col. b. at Griswold, Conn., March 28, 1847. m.
    Lawyer.

CHARLES ROCKWELL LANMAN.   *Cambridge, Mass.*
    Ph.D. b. at Norwich, Conn., July 8, 1850. Prof. of San-
    skrit at Harvard. Pres. Am. Philological Association.
    Projector of the Harvard Oriental Series. Author of
    "Noun-Inflection in the Vedas," "Sanskrit Reader."

ROBERT BRINKLEY LEA.
    b. at Nashville, Tenn., May 7, 1849. m. Lawyer. d. 1895.

HOWARD MANSFIELD   *New York City.*
    M.A., LL B. Col. b. at Hamden, Conn., July 2, 1849.
    Lawyer. Art critic.

ALFRED BISHOP MASON   *New York City.*
    M.A. b. at Bridgeport, Conn., Feb. 23, 1851. m. Man-
    ufacturing and railroad business. One of the translators
    of Von Holst's "Constitutional Hist. of U. S."

ROBERT PEACHY MAYNARD   *Tacoma, Wash.*
    b. at Washington, D. C., July 24, 1849. m. Civil en-
    gineer.

ALBANUS AVERY MOULTON
    M.A. Hillsdale Coll. b. at Roxbury, Mass., Mar. 23, 1848.
    Pres. Rio Grande College. d. 1888.

FRANK MONROE PARSONS
    b. at York, Me., Nov. 6, 1848. m. Lawyer. d. 1877.

WILBERT WARREN PERRY.
    LL.B. Col. b. at Canton, Conn., Dec. 2, 1851. m. Law-
    yer. d. 1895.

HOWARD WALTER POPE.   *New Haven, Conn.*
   B.D.   b. at Westville, Conn., Jan. 21, 1849.   m.   Minister.

WARNER BRADLEY RIGGS   *Dallas, Texas.*
   b. at Macedon, N. Y., Nov. 26, 1849.   m.   Minister.

LUCIUS ADELNO SHERMAN   *Lincoln, Neb.*
   Ph.D.   b. at Douglass, Mass., Aug. 28, 1847.   m.   Prof.
   of English at and Dean of U. of Neb.

JOHN WOLCOTT STARR
   M.A., B.D.   b. at Guilford, Conn., Mar. 8, 1848.   Minister.   d. 1875.

CHARLES EDMUND STEELE   *New Britain, Conn.*
   b. at New Britain, Conn., Nov. 29, 1847.   m.   Market
   gardening and fruit raising business.

GEORGE ARTHUR STRONG   *New York City.*
   b. at Port Gibson, Mich., Oct. 20, 1848.   m.   Lawyer.

THOMAS THACHER   *New York City.*
   M.A., LL.B. Col.   b. at New Haven, Conn., May 3, 1850.
   m.   Lawyer.   Lecturer on Corporate Trusts at Yale.

ALWIN ETHELSTAN TODD
   B.D.   b. at Blanford, Mass.   m.   Minister.   Prof. of Natural Sciences at Berea College.   d. 1897.

NATHAN HART WHITTLESEY   *New Haven, Conn.*
   B.D., D.D. Ill. Coll.   b. at New Preston, Conn., April 19,
   1848.   m.   Minister.

ROBERT EDWARDS WILLIAMS
   C.E. U. of Mich.   b. at Newton, Mass., Jan. 27, 1849.   m.
   Civil engineer.   d. 1887.

EDWARD ALLEN WILSON   *Sierra Mojada, Coahuila, Mexico.*
   Ph.B.   b. at St. Louis, Mo., Aug. 12, 1851.   Mining engineer.

1872

FRANK THURSTON BROWN   *Norwich, Conn.*
   b. at Norwich, Conn., Feb. 27, 1853.   m.   Lawyer.

ROBERT ELMER COE
   b. Dec. 13, 1850.   d. 1872.

OSCAR HENRY COOPER　　　　　　　*Carthage, Texas.*
LL.D. Peabody Coll. m. Teacher.

LEONARD EAGER CURTIS　　　　　　*Englewood, N. J.*
LL.B. b. at Norwalk, O., July 23, 1848. m. Lawyer.

WILLIAM LEE CUSHING　　　　　　*Dobbs Ferry, N. Y.*
M.A. b. at Lee's Island, Phipsburg, Me., July 24, 1849.
m. Head master of Westminster School.

CHARLES ORRIN DAY　　　　　　*Brattleboro, Vt.*
b. at Catskill, N. Y., Nov. 8, 1851. m. Minister.

FRANCIS URQUHART DOWNING　　　　*Columbus, Ga.*
Ph.B., M.E. b. at Columbus, Ga., Dec. 12, 1850. Mechanical engineer.

JOSEPH ALVIN GRAVES　　　　　　*Hartford, Conn.*
Ph.D. b. at Springfield, Mo., Sept. 21, 1849. m. Teacher.

JOHN HOWARD HINCKS
S.T.B. b. at Bucksport, Me., March 19, 1849. Dean of
Atlanta University and Prof. of History and Social
Science. d. 1894.

BENJAMIN HOPPIN　　　　　　*New Haven, Conn.*
b. at Salem, Mass., March 15, 1851. Teacher.

GREENE KENDRICK　　　　　　*Waterbury, Conn.*
LL.B. b. at Waterbury, Conn., May 31, 1851. Lawyer.
Connecticut State Auditor. Mayor of Waterbury.

EDWIN STEVENS LINES　　　　　　*New Haven, Conn.*
D.D. b. at Naugatuck, Conn., Nov. 23, 1845. m. Minister.

EDWARD DeWITT MERRIMAN　　　　*Malone, N. Y.*
b. Aug. 4, 1848. m. Teacher.

GEORGE FOOT MOORE　　　　　　*Andover, Mass.*
M.A., D.D. and Marietta. b. at West Chester, Pa., Oct.
15, 1851. m. Prof. of Hebrew Language and Literature
in Andover Theological Seminary.

JAMES OLMSTEAD
M.D. b. at New Haven, Conn., Nov. 14, 1849. m.
Physician. Supt. of Connecticut Hospital for the Insane.
d. 1897.

EDWARD THOMAS OWEN   *Madison, Wis.*
  b. at Hartford, Conn., March 4, 1850. m. Prof. of French
  at U. of Wis.

GEORGE RICHARDS   *Orange, N. J.*
  M.A., LL.B. Col. b. at Boston, Mass., March 23, 1849.
  m. Lawyer. Author of a book on insurance.

CHARLES JOSEPH HARDY ROPES   *Bangor, Me.*
  D.D., and Bowdoin. b. at St. Petersburg, Russia, Dec. 7,
  1851. m. Theological Professor.

CLEMENT BROOKE WHITE
  b. June 23, 1852. Lawyer. d. 1881.

DAVID JOHNSON HALSTED WILLCOX   *New York City.*
  LL.B. Col. b. at Flatbush, N. Y., Dec. 12, 1849. Lawyer.

1873

EBEN ALEXANDER   *Chapel Hill, N. C.*
  Ph.D. Maryville Coll., LL.D. U. of N. C. b. at Knox-
  ville, Tenn., March 9, 1851. m. Prof. of Greek at U. of
  N. C. Minister to Greece.

ARTHUR HUNTINGTON ALLEN   *Troy, N. Y.*
  b. at New York City, Oct. 20, 1851. m. Minister.

WILLIAM TOWNSEND BARBER   *West Chester, Pa.*
  b. at Baltimore, Md., Dec. 14, 1853. m. Lawyer.

WILLIAM BEEBE   *New Haven, Conn.*
  b. at Litchfield, Conn., Sept. 4, 1851. m. Asst. Prof. of
  Mathematics and Astronomy at Yale. Joint author of
  "Graphic Algebra."

WILLIAM WADE BEEBE
  LL.B. Col. b. at New York City, May 2, 1851. m.
  Lawyer. d. 1886.

ARTHUR BIDDLE
  M.A. b. at Philadelphia, Sept. 23, 1852. m. Lawyer.
  Author of "Treatise on the Law of Warranties in the
  Sales of Chattels," "Law of Insurance." d. 1897.

SALTER STORRS CLARK   *New York City.*
  LL.B. Col. b. at Brooklyn, N. Y., Jan. 10, 1854. m.
  Lawyer.

EDWARD SHEFFIELD COWLES
Ph.D. b. at Farmington, Conn., July 28, 1852. Physician. Teacher. d. 1883.

HERBERT MCKENZIE DENSLOW   *Gambier, O.*
b. at Lynn, Mass., Aug. 20, 1852. m. Lecturer on liturgies and Chaplain of Kenyon College.

EDWARD EVERETT GAYLORD   *Pasadena, Cal.*
M.D. b. at Ashford, Conn., June 6, 1849. m. Physician.

WILLIAM ADDISON HOUGHTON   *Brunswick, Me.*
M.A. b. at Holliston, Mass., March 10, 1852. m. Prof. at University of Japan, Tokio. Prof. of Latin at Bowdoin.

ISAAC NICHOLS JUDSON   *St. Louis, Mo.*
b. at Bridgeport, Conn., July 3, 1853. Teacher.

JAMES ADAM ROBSON   *Canandaigua, N. Y.*
LL.B. Col. b. at Gorham, N. Y., Jan. 1, 1851. Lawyer.

FRANK BIGELOW TARBELL   *Chicago, Ill.*
Ph.D. b. at Groton, Mass., Jan. 1, 1853. Asst. Prof. of Greek at Yale. Director of American School at Athens. Associate Prof. of Greek at U. of Chicago.

FREDERICK CHARLES WEBSTER   *Missoula, Mont.*
b. at Litchfield, Conn., Oct. 17, 1850. m. Lawyer.

1874

EDWARD ALEXANDER BOUCHET   *Philadelphia, Pa.*
Ph.D. b. at New Haven, Conn., Sept. 15, 1852. Teacher.

EDWARD LEWIS CURTIS   *New Haven, Conn.*
Ph.D. Hanover. b. at Ann Arbor, Mich., Oct. 13, 1853. m. Prof. of Old Testament Literature and Exegesis at McCormick Theological Seminary, Chicago.

HENRY WALCOTT FARNAM   *New Haven, Conn.*
R.P.D. Strassburg, M.A. b. at New Haven, Nov. 6, 1853. Prof. of Political Economy at Yale.

THOMAS WILLIAMS GROVER
LL.B. Col. b. at Nashua, N. H., Nov. 29, 1846. m.
Teacher. d. 1893.

DAVID ANDREW KENNEDY *Orange, N. J.*
Ph.D. b. at New York City, March 22, 1851. Teacher.

EDWARD PARMELEE MORRIS *New Haven, Conn.*
M.A. Williams. b. at Auburn, N. Y., Sept. 17, 1853. m.
Prof. of Latin at Williams and Yale.

WILLIAM PARKIN *New York City.*
LL.B. Col. b. at New London, Conn., Sept. 3, 1854.
Lawyer.

JOHN WESLEY PECK *Birmingham, Conn.*
Ph.D. b. at Trumbull, Conn., Feb. 10, 1852. Teacher.

EDWARD DENMORE ROBBINS *Hartford, Conn.*
LL.B. b. at Wethersfield, Conn., Oct. 20, 1853. Lawyer.
Member of Conn. Leg. Member of Conn. State Board
of Education.

ALFRED BEAUMONT THACHER *New York City.*
LL.B. Col. b. at New Haven, Conn., March 22, 1854.
Lawyer.

ARTHUR DEXTER WHITTEMORE *Utica, N. Y.*
b. at Fitzwilliam, N. H., Aug. 11, 1852. m. Dealer in
investment securities.

EDMUND ZACHER *New Haven, Conn.*
LL.B. b. at Hartford, Conn., Dec. 12, 1853. m. Lawyer.

1875.

HENRY BLODGET *Bridgeport, Conn.*
M.D. Bellevue. b. at Greenfield, Mass., Oct. 22, 1854.
Physician.

CHARLES THURSTON CHESTER *Buffalo, N. Y.*
LL.B. Col. b. at Norwich, Conn., Aug. 1, 1853. Lawyer.

HENRY STRONG GULLIVER *Waterbury, Conn.*
M.A., LL.B. Col. b. at Norwich, Conn., Oct. 31, 1853.
Lawyer. Teacher.

JAMES HILLHOUSE   *New York City.*
    LL.B. Col. b. at New Haven, Conn., Nov. 19, 1854.
    Lawyer.

WILLIAM HENRY HOTCHKISS   *Buffalo, N. Y.*
    b. at Bristol, Conn., April 17, 1851. m. Dry goods busi-
    ness.

WILLIAM ROGERS RICHARDS   *Plainfield, N. J.*
    D.D. U. of City of N. Y. b. at Boston, Mass., Dec. 20,
    1853. m. Minister.

CHARLES TRUMBULL RUSS
    LL.B. Col. b. at Hartford, Conn., Jan. 16, 1853. m.
    Lawyer. Life insurance business. d. 1881.

EDWARD WELLS SOUTHWORTH   *New York City.*
    M.L., LL.B. Col. b. Jan. 14, 1854. m. Lawyer.

HAMILTON MERCER WRIGHT   *Bay City, Mich.*
    LL.B. b. at New Orleans, La., Oct. 26, 1851. m. Law-
    yer.

1876

ELISHA SLOCUM BOTTUM
    b. at Norwich, Conn., July 24, 1854. m. Lawyer.
    Assistant State Att'y of Ill. d. 1898.

DAVID WALTER BROWN   *New York City.*
    Ph.D. b. at Ogdensburg, N. Y., Aug. 10, 1852. Assistant
    Editor of the "Sanitary Engineer." Author of "A Brief
    History of American Patent Legislation," "The American
    Patent System."

GEORGE ENSIGN BUSHNELL   *Fort Hamilton, N. Y.*
    Ph.D., M.D. b. at Worcester, Mass., Sept. 10, 1853. m.
    Captain and Assistant Surgeon in United States Army.

GEORGE EATON CONEY   *New York City.*
    LL.B. Col. b. at Newark, O., May 2, 1856. m. Lawyer.

FRANKLIN AUGUSTUS GAYLORD   *New York City.*
    b. at Yonkers, N. Y., May 1, 1856. m. Preacher.
    Teacher. General Sec'y of the French Young Men's
    Christian Association of Paris, France.

JOHN BLANCHARD GLEASON   *New York City.*
  b. at Delhi, N. Y., Aug. 19, 1855. m. Lawyer.

ARTHUR TWINING HADLEY   *New Haven, Conn.*
  M.A. b. at New Haven, Conn., April 23, 1856. m. Prof.
  of Political Science at Yale. Commissioner of Labor
  Statistics of the State of Conn. 1885–87. Author of " Rail-
  way Transportation ; its History and its Laws."

WILLIAM WALDO HYDE   *Hartford, Conn.*
  LL.B. Boston. b. at Tolland, Conn., March 25, 1854. m.
  Lawyer. Mayor of Hartford.

JOHN B. KENDRICK   *Wallingford, Conn.*
  b. at Washington, Conn., Sept. 18, 1851. m. Teacher.

MYRON HENRY PHELPS   *New York City.*
  LL.B. Columbian U. and Col. b. at Lewiston, Ill., April
  2, 1856. m. Lawyer.

GEORGE WILLIAM ROLLINS   *Boston, Mass.*
  b. at Geneva, N. Y., Feb. 19, 1834. m. Teacher.

LEVERITT HYSLIP SAGE   *Hackensack, N. J.*
  b. at Brooklyn, N. Y., Oct. 22, 1855. Commercial travel-
  ler.

CHARLES HENRY WILLCOX   *Lawrenceville, N. J.*
  B.D. b. at Fitchburg, Mass., May 11, 1855. m. Minister.
  Teacher.

EDWIN DEAN WORCESTER   *New York City.*
  LL.B. b. at Albany, N. Y., Feb. 25, 1856. Lawyer.

1877

JOHN BIRDSYE ATWATER   *Minneapolis, Minn.*
  b. at Minneapolis, Minn., March 23, 1885. m. Lawyer.

CHARLES CLARK CAMP   *Faribault, Minn.*
  b. at Meriden, Conn., Dec. 4, 1855. Minister.

CLEAVELAND FORBES   *San Francisco, Cal.*
  LL.B. Col. b. at San Francisco, Cal., Feb. 5, 1858. Civil
  engineer.

THOMAS DWIGHT GOODELL   *New Haven, Conn.*
  Ph.D. b. at Ellington, Conn., Nov. 8, 1854. m. Asst.
  Prof. of Greek at Yale. Author of articles in the Trans-
  actions of Am. Philological Ass'n.

WEBSTER MERRIFIELD   *University, N. Dakota.*
M.A.   b. at Williamsville, Vt., July 27, 1852.   President
of U. of North Dakota.

FREDERICK BOSWORTH PERCY   *Brookline, Mass.*
M.D. Homeopathic School, Boston.   b. at Bath, Me., July
23, 1856.   m.   Prof. of Materia Medica at Boston U.

JOSEPH GILPIN PYLE   *St. Paul, Minn.*
b. at Calvert, Md., May 14, 1853.   m.   Associate editor of
the St. Paul Pioneer Press.   Author of "The Little Cryp-
togam," "The Resources and Industries of Minnesota."

ORRAY TAFT SHERMAN   *Nyack, N. Y.*
b. at Providence, R. I., Aug. 5, 1856.   Scientific Investi-
gator and Explorer.   Author of numerous articles on
scientific subjects.

MORRIS SHOTWELL SHIPLEY
b. at Cincinnati, O., Dec. 7, 1856.   m.   Manufacturing
business.   d. 1898.

JOHN SEYMOUR THACHER   *New York City.*
M.D. P. and S.   b. at New Haven, Conn., June 10, 1856.
Physician.   Lecturer on Pathology and Clinical Medicine
at New York Polyclinic.   Pathologist to the Presbyterian
Hospital and St. Luke's Hospital.

ALEXANDER MARTIN WILCOX   *Lawrence, Kan.*
Ph.D.   b. at Baltimore, Md., June 19, 1849.   m.   Prof. of
Greek in U. of Kansas.

1878

WILLIAM MARTIN ABER   *Missoula, Mont.*
b. at Sparta, N. Y., May 29, 1848.   m.   Prof. at Utah U.

HARLAN PAGE BEACH   *Springfield, Mass.*
b. at South Orange, N. J., May 4, 1854.   m.   Missionary.

FRANK ARMSTRONG BECKWITH
M.D. Harv.   b. at Honolulu, H. I., April 23, 1854.   m.
Minister.   d. 1885.

DOUGLAS PUTNAM BIRNIE   *Boston, Mass.*
b. at Springfield, Mass., Sept. 3, 1856.   Minister.

HOLLIS WILLIAM COBB   *Worcester, Mass.*
    b. at Boylston, Mass., March 14, 1856. Lawyer.

HENRY CLARK COE   *New York City.*
    M.A., M.D. Harv. and P. and S. b. at Cincinnati, O., 1856.
    m. Physician. Member of Royal College of Surgeons.
    Licentiate of Royal College of Physicians.

GEORGE LOUIS CURTIS   *Baltimore, Md.*
    b. at Adrian, Mich., May 21, 1855. Commandant of
    "Hampton Normal and Agricultural Institute for Negroes
    and Indians." Minister.

STANLEY WALKER DEXTER   *New York City.*
    b. at London, Eng., Oct. 3, 1857. m. Lawyer.

BURGESS SCOTT HURTT
    b. at Cincinnati, O., Dec. 6, 1856. Business. d. 1888.

JOHN GOULD JENNINGS   *Cleveland, O.*
    b. at Cleveland, O., Sept. 28, 1856. m. Manufacturer.

CLARENCE HILL KELSEY   *New York City.*
    M.A. b. at Bridgeport, Conn., Dec. 23, 1856. m. Lawyer.

GEORGE TAPSCOTT KNOTT   *Wichita Falls, Texas.*
    b. at Clifton, O., March 14, 1855. Real estate business.

GEORGE SMITH PALMER   *Norwich, Conn.*
    b. at Montville, Conn., March 20, 1855. m. Manufac-
    turer.

CHARLES PARSONS   *New York City.*
    b. at Savannah, Ga., Jan. 18, 1858. m. Railroad business.

ALFRED LAWRENCE RIPLEY   *Boston, Mass.*
    M.A. b. at Hartford, Conn., Nov. 6, 1858. Banking
    business.

EDWARD HOWARD SEELY
    LL.B. Col. b. at Brooklyn, N. Y. Author of " A Lone
    Star, Bo Peep," "A Nymph of the West." d. 1894.

CHARLES SIDNEY SHEPARD   *Buffalo, N. Y.*
    LL.B Harv. b. at Buffalo, N. Y., July 29, 1856. Manu-
    facturing business.

WILLIAM HOWARD TAFT   *Cincinnati, O.*
    LL.D. b. at Cincinnati, O., Sept. 15, 1857. m. Lawyer.
    Collector of Internal Revenue. Judge of Superior Court
    of Cincinnati, and U. S. Circuit Court.

WILLIAM EVERETT WATERS　　　　　*Aurora, N. Y.*
　　Ph.D.　b. at Winthrop, Me., Dec. 20, 1856.　m.　Prof. of
　　Greek at U. of Cincinnati.　President of Wells College.

1879

RALPH BARKER　　　　　*Madison, Fla.*
　　b. at Brooklyn, N. Y., Aug. 26, 1857.　m.　Cotton business.

LOUIS NORMAN BOOTH　　　　　*Bridgeport, Conn.*
　　b. at Bridgeport, Conn., March 4, 1859.　m.　Minister.

LLOYD WHEATON BOWERS　　　　　*Chicago, Ill.*
　　LL.B. Col.　b. at Springfield, Mass., March 9, 1859.
　　Lawyer.

LUCIEN FRANCIS BURPEE　　　　　*Waterbury, Conn.*
　　b. at Rockville, Conn., Oct. 12, 1855.　m.　Lawyer.　City
　　Att'y of Waterbury.

ERNEST CARTER　　　　　*New York City.*
　　b. at Galena, Ill., Jan. 12, 1858.　Lawyer.

AARON VAN SCHAICK COCHRANE　　　　　*Hudson, N. Y.*
　　b. at Coxsackie, N. Y., March 14, 1858.　m.　Lawyer.

HENRY COOPER CROUCH　　　　　*Colorado Springs, Col.*
　　M.A.　b. at Galena, Ill., March 11, 1858.　Teacher.

JOHN VILLIERS FARWELL　　　　　*Chicago, Ill.*
　　b. at Chicago, Ill., Oct. 16, 1858.　m.　Wholesale dry
　　goods business.

GEORGE FORRIS FOSTER　　　　　*New York City.*
　　b. at Grand Rapids, Mich., Oct. 22, 1856.　Journalist.

SAMUEL MONELL FOSTER　　　　　*Fort Wayne, Ind.*
　　b. at Coldenham, N. Y., Dec. 12, 1851.　m.　Dry goods
　　business.

JOHN MILTON FOX　　　　　*Kansas City, Mo.*
　　LL.B. Columbian U.　b. at East Lynne, Conn., Sept. 9,
　　1853.　m.　Lawyer.

JOHN LESTER FRANKLIN　　　　　*Buffalo, N. Y.*
　　B.D.　b. at New Haven, Conn., March 19, 1856.　Minister.

ROBERT RYERS GRISWOLD   *Binghamton, N. Y.*
    b. at Binghamton, N. Y., July 20, 1856. m. Lumber
business.

MALCOLM McIVOR McKENZIE   *New Haven, Conn.*
    b. at St. Paul, Minn., Oct. 12, 1857.

IVAN MATTHIAS MARTY
    b. at Monroe, Wis., Sept. 14, 1856. m. Minister. d. 1889.

EDWARD McARTHUR NOYES   *Newton Centre, Mass.*
    B.D. b. at New Haven, Conn., Oct. 12, 1858. m. Min-
ister

THOMAS EDWARD ROCHFORT
    LL.B. Columbian U. b. at New Haven, Conn., Aug. 30,
1857. Lawyer. d. 1894.

LOUIS LEE STANTON   *New York City.*
    b. at Stonington, Conn., July 31, 1859. m. Iron manu-
facturer.

HENRY JAMES TEN EYCK
    b. at Albany, N. Y., July 25, 1856. Journalist. d. 1887.

AMBROSE TIGHE   *St. Paul, Minn.*
    M.A. b. at Brooklyn, N. Y., May 8, 1859. Teacher.
Lawyer.

OTIS HARVEY WALDO   *Chicago, Ill.*
    b. at Milwaukee, Wis., Nov. 11, 1857. m. Lawyer.

1880.

JOHN ARNOLD AMUNDSON   *New York City.*
    LL.B. b. at Madison, Wis., April 2, 1856. m. Lawyer.

EDWARD MANROSS BENTLEY   *New York City.*
    b. at Ellenville, N. Y., July 31, 1858. m. Specialist in
the Law of Electrical Patents.

WALTER HULL BUELL   *Scranton, Pa.*
    M.A. b. at Killingworth, Conn., Aug. 27, 1858. m.
Teacher.

JOHN EDWARD BUSHNELL   *New York City.*
    B.D. b. at Old Saybrook, Conn., Oct. 21, 1858. m.
Minister.

FRANK GOODRICH   *Williamstown, Mass.*
  Ph.D. Halle. b. at Dryden, N. Y., April 21, 1856. m.
  Prof. of German Language and History at Williams.

EDMUND FRANK GREEN   *New York City.*
  LL.B. Col. b. at Corunna, Mich., April 3, 1857. Real
  estate business.

WILLIAM MONTAGUE HALL
  b. at New York City, July 2, 1857. Prof. Political and
  Social Science at Colorado Coll. d. 1894.

FRANKLIN WHETSONE HOPKINS   *New York City.*
  M.A. b. at Cincinnati, O., Dec. 2, 1857. m. Banker.

FREDERICK STILLMAN MORRISON   *Hartford, Conn.*
  b. at Berlin, Conn., Oct. 20, 1858. m. Teacher.

ALFRED BULL NICHOLS   *Cambridge, Mass.*
  B.D. Cambr. Episc. Theol. School. b. at Lebanon, Conn.,
  July 7, 1852. Instructor in German at Harvard.

DICKINSON WOODRUFF RICHARDS   *New York City.*
  LL.B. Col. b. at Boston, Mass., Nov. 30, 1858. m. Lawyer.

WILLIAM HAZARD SHERMAN
  b. at New York City, July 14, 1859. Surgeon. d. 1893.

FREDERICK MORSE SMITH   *Hartford, Conn.*
  M.A. Harv. b. at Glastonbury, Conn., Nov. 20, 1858.
  Home missionary.

GRANT ALEXANDER SMITH
  b. at Fox Lake, Wis., Feb. 27, 1859. m. Wholesale grocery business. d. 1887.

ARTHUR EUGENE WALRADT   *New York City.*
  LL.B. b. at Northbridge, Mass., Jan. 3, 1859. m. Lawyer.

WILSON CURTISS WHEELER   *Chapman, Kan.*
  B.D. b. at Huntington, Mass., May 23, 1857. m. Minister.

HEMAN CHARLES WHITTLESEY   *Middletown, Conn.*
  b. at Newington, Conn., Jan. 4, 1857. Assistant in the
  Chinese Customs Service.
  6

1881

EDWIN EDGERTON AIKEN　　　　　　　　*Tientsin, China.*
B.D. b. in 1859. Missionary.

PHILIP GOLDEN BARTLETT　　　　　　　*New York City.*
b. in 1860. Lawyer.

RUSSELL ANSON BIGELOW
LL.B. Col. b. in 1859. Lawyer. d. 1890.

ARTHUR ELMORE BOSTWICK　　　　　　*Montclair, N. J.*
Ph.D. b. in 1860. m. Member of editorial staff of Appleton's Cyclopædia of American Biography. Librarian.

WALTER RAY BRIDGMAN　　　　　　　*Lake Forest, Ill.*
M.A. and Miami. b. in 1860. Prof. of Greek at Miami and Lake Forest.

LEVI ABRAHAM ELIEL　　　　　　　　*Chicago, Ill.*
b. in 1859. Lawyer.

NATHANIEL TAYLOR GUERNSEY　　　　*Des Moines, Iowa.*
LL.B. b. in 1858. Lawyer.

WILLIAM BURR HILL　　　　　　　　*New York City.*
LL.B. b. in 1857. Teacher.

CHARLES WITTENBERG HOLZHEIMER
b. in 1861. m. Lawyer. d. 1888.

GEORGE EDWARD IDE　　　　　　　*Brooklyn, N. Y.*
b. in 1860. m. Broker.

JAMES LEIGHTON
b. at Abington, Pa., May 2, 1859. d. 1883.

FRANK BENJAMIN LUCAS　　　　　　*New York City.*
b. in 1858. Life insurance business.

ISAAC THOMAS　　　　　　　　　*New Haven, Conn.*
M.A. b. in 1849. m. Teacher.

ADRIAN SEBASTIAN VAN DE GRAAFF　　*Tuscaloosa, Ala.*
b. in 1859. Prof. of Law at U. of Ala.

ARTHUR ELI WHITE　　　　　　　*New York City.*
Teacher.

1882

FRANK FROST ABBOTT   *Chicago, Ill.*
   Ph.D. b. in 1860. m. Prof. of Latin at U. of Chicago.

MORGAN HAWLEY BEACH   *Alexandria, Va.*
   B.L. U. of Va. b. in 1862. Lawyer.

JOHN REMSEN BISHOP   *Cincinnati, O.*
   m. Teacher.

CHARLES EDWARD BLUMLEY   *Norwich, Conn.*
   b. in 1856. Lawyer.

BENJAMIN BREWSTER   *New York City.*
   B.D. Gen. Theol. Sem. b. in 1861. Minister.

WAYLAND IRVING BRUCE   *Easthampton, Mass.*
   M.A. b. in 1858. m. Teacher.

EDWARD BRADFORD CRAGIN   *New York City.*
   M.D. P. and S. b. in 1860. Physician.

CHARLES BURR GRAVES   *New London, Conn.*
   M.D. Harv. b. in 1860. Physician.

BARCLAY JOHNSON
   b. in 1862. Lawyer. d. 1885.

JULIUS HOWARD PRATT   *Milwaukee, Wis.*
   Ph.D. b. in 1861. Teacher.

DANIEL SAMMIS SANFORD   *Brookline, Mass.*
   M.A. b. in 1859. Teacher.

WILLIAM SEYMOUR   *Chicago, Ill.*
   m. Carriage business.

JOHN LEWIS WELLS   *Ipswich, South Dakota.*
   b. in 1861. m. Lawyer.

FRANKLIN ELDRED WORCESTER
   Ph.B. and M.E. b. in 1861. Railroad business. d. 1891.

1883

EDWARD INCREASE BOSWORTH   *Oberlin, O.*
   B.D. Oberlin. b. 1861. Minister. Prof. of English
   Bible at Oberlin.

EDWARD GAYLORD BOURNE   *New Haven, Conn.*
Ph.D. b. 1860. Prof. of History at W. Reserve. Prof. of History at Yale. Author of "The History of the Surplus Revenue of 1837."

ARTHUR EUGENE BOWERS   *Manchester, Conn.*
b. 1856. Journalist.

AUSTIN LORD BOWMAN   *Roanoke, Va.*
b. 1862. Teacher.

WOOLSEY CARMALT   *New York City.*
LL.B. Col. b. 1863. Lawyer.

GEORGE PRENTISS CARROLL   *Bridgeport, Conn.*
LL.B. Boston U. b. 1861. Lawyer.

ARTHUR BRADFORD CORNWALL   *New York City.*
b. 1862. Banking business.

EVERETT JAMES ESSELSTYN   *New York City.*
LL.B. Col. b. 1861. Teacher. Lawyer.

STEPHEN LEONARD GEISTHARDT   *Lincoln, Neb.*
LL.B. Col. b 1862. Lawyer.

WILLIAM IRWIN GRUBB   *Birmingham, Ala.*
b. 1862. Lawyer.

GEORGE WASHINGTON JOHNSTON   *Cincinnati, O.*
b. 1862. Real estate business.

FRED WILLIAM KELLOGG
b. 1861. Teacher. d. 1883.

CLIFFORD STEPHEN KELSEY   *New York City.*
b. 1860. Civil engineer.

CHARLES MARTIN KENDALL   *Denver, Col.*
b. 1860. Lawyer.

CARLL ANDREWS LEWIS   *Elliot, Conn.*
b. 1862. m. Teacher.

JOSEPH MCKEEN LEWIS
b. 1863. Teacher. d. 1887.

ALLYN COOK LOOMIS
b. 1861. Teacher. d. 1884.

EDWARD TOMPKINS MCLAUGHLIN
  b. 1860. m. Asst. Prof. of English and Prof. of Rhetoric and Belles Lettres at Yale. d. 1893.

ELIAKIM HASTINGS MOORE	*Chicago, Ill.*
  Ph.D. b. 1862. Prof. of Math. at U. of Chicago.

SAMUEL BALL PLATNER	*Cleveland, O.*
  Ph.D. b. 1863. Prof. of Latin at W. Reserve. Member of American Philological Association, and of American Oriental Society.

WILLIAM PRICE	*Pottstown, Pa.*
  b. 1860. Prof. French at Trinity, N. C.

CHARLES COLEBROOK SHERMAN	*Chicago, Ill.*
  b. 1861. Teacher.

THOMAS SHEPARD SOUTHWORTH	*New York City.*
  M.D. P. and S. b. 1861. Physician.

HORACE DUTTON TAFT	*Watertown, Conn.*
  M.A. b. 1862. Teacher.

1884

FREDERICK STURGES ALLEN	*New York City.*
  b. 1861. Lawyer. Author of "Ancients for Little Moderns."

FRANK OLIVER AYRES	*New York City.*
  b. 1862. Lawyer.

CHARLES EDWIN BEDELL	*New York City.*
  b. 1862. m. Civil engineer.

GEORGE REDDINGTON BLODGETT
  b. 1862. m. Lawyer. d. 1897.

WILBUR FRANKLIN BOOTH	*Minneapolis, Minn.*
  LL.B. b. 1861. Lawyer.

ROBERT MUNRO BOYD	*Montclair, N. J.*
  LL.B., M.A. Col. b. 1863. Lawyer.

CHARLES EUGENE CARR
  b. 1863. Teacher. d. 1888.

EDWARD MORTIMER CHAPMAN	*Worcester, Mass.*
  B.D. b. 1862. m. Minister.

EDWARD CHENERY GALE *Minneapolis, Minn.*
M.A. Harv. b. 1862. m. Lawyer.

GUSTAV GRUENER *New Haven, Conn.*
Ph.D. b. 1863. Prof. of German at Yale.

JAMES SMITH HAVENS *Rochester, N. Y.*
b. 1859. m. Lawyer.

RODERICK WHITTELSEY HINE *Dedham, Mass.*
b. 1859. m. Supt. of Schools.

FREDERICK SCHEETZ JONES *Minneapolis, Minn.*
M.A. b. 1862. m. Prof. of Physics and Electricity at
U. of Minn.

DAVID KINLEY *Urbana, Ill.*
Ph.D. U. of Wis. b. 1861. Prof. of Political Economy
and Social Science at U. of Ill.

EDWARD ASHTON LAWRENCE
b. at Prairie City, Ill., July 25, 1861. d. 1884.

CHARLES ABERNETHY MEAD *Orange, N. J.*
b. 1862. Teacher.

WILLIAM THEOPHILUS NICHOLS *New York City.*
b. 1863. Journalist.

FRANK DUNLAP PAVEY *New York City.*
LL.B. and M.L. b. 1860. Lawyer.

BENJAMIN SCHARPS *New York City.*
b. 1864. Lawyer.

JOHN IRA SOUTHER *Chicago, Ill.*
b. 1861. m. Chemist.

SELDEN PALMER SPENCER *St. Louis, Mo.*
b. 1862. m. Lawyer.

SYDNEY STEIN *Chicago, Ill.*
b. 1862. Lawyer.

HENRY BANCROFT TWOMBLY *Summit, N. J.*
b. 1862. m. Lawyer.

DEAN AUGUSTUS WALKER *Aurora, N. Y.*
B.D. and M.A. b. 1860. Fellow and Lecturer at U. of
Chicago. Prof. of English Bible at Wells College.

HENRY MILTON WOLFE *Chicago, Ill.*
b. 1860. Lawyer.

1885

JONATHAN BARNES   *Springfield, Mass.*
  b. 1865. Lawyer.

JOHN HENRY BOOTH   *Plattsburgh, N. Y.*
  LL.B. Col. b. 1864. m. Lawyer.

JOHN CLOYSE BRIDGMAN   *Wilkes Barre, Pa.*
  b. 1863. Manufacturing business.

CHARLES LYMAN CARHART   *Marlboro, N.Y.*
  b. 1865. Minister.

WILBUR LUCIUS CROSS   *New Haven, Conn.*
  Ph.D. b. 1862. m. Instructor in English at Yale.

HERBERT LIONEL DOGGETT
  b. at Iowa City, Ia., Nov. 15, 1863. Lawyer. d. 1894.

JOHN DENNIS FERRIS   *Chatham, N. J.*
  b. 1862. Engineer.

WALTER FRANCIS FREAR   *Honolulu, H. I.*
  LL.B. b. 1863. m. Lawyer. Second associate justice
  of the Supreme Court of Hawaii.

EDWARD AUGUSTUS GEORGE   *Willimantic, Conn.*
  M.A., B.D. b. 1865. m. Minister.

EDWARD NEBLETT HIDDEN   *St. Louis, Mo.*
  b. 1860. Lawyer. Business.

JAMES RICHARD JOY   *New York City.*
  M.A. b. 1863. m. Editor. Author of "Essay on the
  Greek Drama," "Outline History of Greece," "Outline
  History of Rome," "Outline History of England," and
  "Rome and the Making of Modern Europe."

GUY WARD MALLON   *Cincinnati, O.*
  b. 1864. Lawyer. Member of Ohio Leg.

WILLIAM PROCTER MORRISON   *Cincinnati, O.*
  b. 1862. Manufacturing business.

EUGENE LAMB RICHARDS   *New York City.*
  b. 1863. Lawyer.

GEORGE EDGAR VINCENT   *Chicago, Ill.*
  b. 1864. m. Asst. Prof. of Sociology at U. of Chicago.

PAUL IRVING WELLES   *Columbia, S. C.*
   b. 1863.   m.   Railroad business.

HERBERT HENRY WHITE
   M.A.   b. at New Haven, Conn., Nov. 16, 1861.   Prof. of
Latin and Greek at Gates Coll.   d. 1893.

LEVI OLMSTEAD WIGGINS
   M.D. P. and S.   b. at Newburgh, N. Y., Oct. 31, 1865.
Physician.   d. 1891.

WILFRED JAMES WORCESTER   *New York City.*
   b. 1864.

1886

ARTHUR NATHANIEL ALLING   *New Haven, Conn.*
   M.D. P and S.   b. at New Haven, Conn., July 1, 1862.
m.   Asst. instructor in Ophthalmology at Yale Medical
School.   Chief of Ophthalmological Clinic in New
Haven Dispensary.

WILLIAM ADAMS BROWN   *New York City.*
   M.A.   b. at New York City, Dec. 29, 1865.   m.   Prof. of
Systematic Theology at Union Seminary.   Author
of " Musical Instruments and their Homes."

CARL DARLING BUCK   *Chicago, Ill.*
   Ph.D.   b. at Orland, Me., Oct. 2, 1866.   m.   Prof. of
Indo-European Comparative Philology at U. of Chicago.
Member of Oriental Society and of Am. Philological
Society.   Author of " Der Vocalismus der Oskischen
Sprache "; an editor of "Studies in Classical Philology."

JOHN JOSEPH CORKERY   *Norwich, Conn.*
   b. at Norwich, Conn., March 20, 1863.   Lawyer.

BENJAMIN JOSEPH DAVIS   *Easton, Pa.*
   b. at Hamden, Conn., Oct. 28, 1864.   m.   Minister.

CALVIN DICKEY   *Chicago, Ill.*
   M.A.   b. at Newark, O., Jan. 12, 1863.   Real estate business.

JUDSON SCHULTZE DUTCHER   *Watertown, Conn.*
   b. at Ellenville, N. Y., Dec. 18, 1862.   Teacher.

GEORGE EDWIN ELIOT *Clinton, Conn.*
M.A. b. at Clinton, Conn., June 1, 1864. Teacher.

ARTHUR GOEBEL *Covington, Ky.*
b. at Carbondale, Pa., March 22, 1863. Carpet business.

CHAUNCEY WILLIAM GOODRICH *Orange, N.J.*
b. at Cleveland, O., Nov. 17, 1846. m. Minister.

WASHINGTON IRVING HUNT
Ph.D. b. at Ellington, N. Y., Nov. 17, 1864. m. Teacher.
Author of "Notes on the Battle Field of Plataea,"
"Homeric Wit and Humour." d. 1893.

HERBERT ARMSTRONG JAGGARD *Downingtown, Pa.*
C.E. Rensselaer Polytechnical Inst. b. at Altoona, Pa.,
Jan. 22, 1865. Civil engineer.

CHARLTON MINER LEWIS *New Haven, Conn.*
LL.B. Col. b. at Brooklyn, N. Y., March 4, 1866.
Instructor in English at Yale.

CHARLES ALBERT MOORE *Rockland, Me.*
b. at West Chester, Pa., July 6, 1864. m. Minister.

FRANK GARDNER MOORE *Hanover, N. H.*
Ph.D. b. at West Chester, Pa., Sept. 25, 1865. m. Asst.
Prof. of Latin at Dartmouth. Author of articles in
Transactions of the American Philological Association.

WILLIAM HENRY PARKS *Paris, France.*
Ph.D. b. at Clinton, Conn., Nov. 6, 1864. Business.

ARTHUR STEVENS PHELPS *Greeley, Col.*
B.D. b. at New Haven, Conn., Jan. 23, 1863. m. Minister.

CHARLES WHEELER PIERSON *New York City.*
M.A. b. at Florida, N. Y., May 3, 1864. Lawyer.

EDWARD WINTHROP REID
b. at. Syracuse, N. Y., Dec. 19, 1864. d. 1885.

JOHN CHRISTOPHER SCHWAB *New Haven, Conn.*
M.A., Ph.D. Goettingen. b. at Fordham Heights, N. Y.,
April 1, 1865. m. Asst. Prof. of Economics at Yale
Author of articles in Yale Review, and in publications of
American Economic Association.

1887

JAMES ARCHBALD   *Scranton, Pa.*
b. at Scranton, Pa., Feb. 19, 1866. Coal business.

WILLOUGHBY MAYNARD BABCOCK   *Minneapolis, Minn.*
LL.B. b. at Hanover, N. Y., Oct. 28, 1864. m. Lawyer.

GERALD HAMILTON BEARD   *South Norwalk, Conn.*
B.D., Ph.D. b. at Hammersmith, Eng., March 20, 1862.
m. Minister.

JOHN BENNETTO
M.A., LL.B., b. at Pool, Eng., Jan. 22, 1862. Lawyer.
d. 1892.

EDWARD LYDSTON BLISS   *Foo Chow, China.*
M.D. b. at Newburyport, Mass., Dec. 10, 1865. Asst.
in Chem. at Yale.

CARLETON LEWIS BROWNSON   *New York City.*
b. at New Canaan, Conn., Jan. 19, 1866. m. Teacher.

WILLIAM SAVAGE BURNS   *Bath, N. Y.*
B.L.S. U. of State of N. Y. b. at Litchfield, Ill., Jan. 18,
1866. Librarian.

WILLIAM AARON CORNISH   *Gillette, N. J.*
b. at Gillette, N. J., Nov. 2, 1862. m. Teacher.

JOHN HUBBARD CURTIS
b. at Hartford, Conn., June 9, 1865. Teacher. d. 1897.

THOMAS HAMLIN CURTIS   *New Haven, Conn.*
b. at Hallowell, Me., May 9, 1866. Engineer.

JOHN CASPAR DIEHL   *Erie, Pa.*
b. at Erie, Pa., Jan. 12, 1865. Principal of High School.

HARRY BURR FERRIS   *New Haven, Conn.*
M.D. b. at Greenwich, Conn., May 21, 1865. m. Physician and Prof. of Anatomy at Yale.

WILLIAM JESSUP HAND   *Scranton, Pa*
b. at Scranton, Pa., July 26, 1866. m. Lawyer.

FREDERIC WELLS HART   *La Junta, Col.*
b. at Plainville, Conn., July 12, 1866. m. Minister.

ROBERT IRVING JENKS   *New York City.*
   b. at Cincinnati, O., Jan. 15, 1865.   Business.

YAN PHOU LEE
   b. at Fragrant Hills, China, 1861.   m.   Business.

HARRY LYNE   *Denver, Col.*
   b. at Augusta, Ill., July 11, 1856.   m.   Ore buyer for
   smelter.

GEORGE DANIEL PETTEE   .   *Andover, Mass.*
   b. at Sharon, Mass., July 24, 1864.   m.   Teacher.   Registrar of the Faculty at Phillips Academy.

WILLIAM LYON PHELPS   *New Haven, Conn.*
   Ph.D., M.A. Harv.   b. at New Haven, Conn., Jan. 2, 1865.
   m.   Asst. Prof. of English at Yale.   Author of "The Be-
   ginnings of the English Romantic Movement."   Editor
   of "Gray's Works."

JOHN NORTON POMEROY   *San Francisco, Cal.*
   M.A., LL.B., U. of Cal.   b. at South Orange, N. J., May
   7, 1866.   Lawyer.   Joint editor of "Pomeroy's Equity
   Jurisprudence."   Editor "Pomeroy on Remedies."

EDWARD TALLMADGE ROOT   *Providence, R. I.*
   B.D.   b. at Springfield, O., March 19, 1865.   m.   Minister.

GRANT ISAAC ROSENZWEIG   *Kansas City, Mo.*
   b. at Erie, Pa., Sept. 15, 1865.   m.   Lawyer.

WILLIAM ALBERT SETCHELL   *Berkeley, Cal.*
   M.A., Ph.D. Harv.   b. at Norwich, Conn., April 15, 1864.
   Professor of Botany at Univ. of Cal.   Author of botani-
   cal papers.

FREDERIC ROGER WHITTLESEY   *New York City.*
   b. at Southington, Conn., July 12, 1865.   m.   Business.

1888

EDWARD FRANCIS AYRES
   M.A., LL.B. Columbian U.   b. at New Canaan, Conn.,
   Jan. 19, 1866.   m.   Lawyer.   d. 1894.

WILLIAM PITT BALDWIN   *New Haven, Conn.*
   M.D. and N. Y. Homœopathic Coll.   b. at New Haven,
   Conn., May 12, 1867.   Physician.

JESSE HATCH BEHRENDS · *Buffalo, N. Y.*
b. at Yonkers, N. Y., May 8, 1867. m. Lawyer.

HENRY BARNARD BROWNELL *New York City.*
LL.B. and LL.M. Georgetown. b. at East Orange, N. J.,
Nov. 8, 1865. Lawyer.

· JOHN FRANKLIN CARTER *Fall River, Mass.*
B.D. Cambridge Episc. Theol. School. b. at Orange, N. J.,
Oct. 21, 1864. m. Minister.

HARLAN WARD COOLEY *Chicago, Ill.*
b. at Washington, D. C., Jan. 29, 1866. m. Lawyer.

CHARLES EDWARD CORNWALL *New Haven, Conn.*
b. at New Haven, Conn., July 1, 1867. Banking business.

EDWARD THOMAS FARRINGTON
M.D. P. and S. b. at Brooklyn, N. Y., Feb. 26, 1866. m.
Physician. d. 1896.

EDWARD COLTON FELLOWES *Derby, Conn.*
B.D. b. at Hartford, Conn., Feb. 22, 1864. m. Minister.

IRVING FISHER *New Haven, Conn.*
Ph.D. b. at Saugerties, N. Y., Feb. 27, 1867. m. Asst.
Prof. of Political Science at Yale. Translator and editor
of Prof. Walras' "Geometrical Theory of the Determina-
tion of Prices."

DANIEL BAILEY HARDENBERGH *New York City.*
M.D. P. and S. b. at Port Jervis, N. Y., March 13, 1866.
Physician.

ORLAND SIDNEY ISBELL *Denver, Col.*
LL.B. b. at Bridgeport, Conn., Nov. 19, 1866. Lawyer.

THEODORE LOCKWOOD LEVERETT *Parowan, Utah.*
b. at New York City, Oct. 8, 1867. Minister.

WILLIAM LORING *St. Joseph, Mo.*
b. at St. Joseph, Mo., Aug. 12, 1867. Wholesale drug
business.

HENRY WEBER MCCAULEY *Reading, Pa.*
b. at Reading, Pa., Nov. 3, 1865.

HAROLD VAN METER OGDEN *Olympia, Wash.*
b. at Charleston, Ill., Nov. 24, 1866. m. Lumber business.

HARRISON GRAY PLATT   *Portland, Ore.*
   b. at Milford, Conn., Aug. 24, 1866. m. Lawyer.

FRED PALMER SOLLEY   *New York City.*
   Ph.B., M.D. P. and S. b. at Newark, N. J., Oct. 10, 1866.
   m. Physician.

BERNARD CHRISTIAN STEINER   *Baltimore, Md.*
   M.A., Ph.D. Johns Hopkins, LL.B. U. of Md. b. at Guil-
   ford, Conn., Aug. 3, 1867. Librarian of the Enoch Pratt
   Free Library of Baltimore.

HENRY EBENEZER STEVENS   *New York City.*
   b. at New York City, June 14, 1866. m. Lumber business.

HENRY LEWIS STIMSON   *New York City.*
   M.A. Harv. b. at New York City, Sept. 21, 1867. m.
   Lawyer.

HERBERT CUSHING TOLMAN   *Nashville, Tenn.*
   Ph.D. b. at South Scituate, Mass., Nov. 4, 1865. m.
   Prof. of Greek at U. of N. C. and Vanderbilt Univ. Fellow of the Royal Asiatic Society. Author of "Old Persian Grammar," "Cæsar's Gallic War," "Gospel of Matthew in Greek," "Guide to the Ancient Persian Cunei-
   form Inscriptions," "Latin Text of the Gallic War,"
   "Greek and Roman Mythology."

1889

WILLIAM POPE AIKEN   *New York City.*
   LL.B. b. at Newington, Conn., Feb. 1, 1866. Lawyer.

JOHN WALLACE BANKS   *Bridgeport, Conn.*
   LL.B. b. at Bethlehem, Conn., Sept. 22, 1867. Lawyer.

LESTER BRADNER   *New York City.*
   Ph.D., B.D. Gen. Theol. Sem. b. at Chicago, Ill., March
   9, 1867. m. Minister.

GEORGE COGGILL   *New York City.*
   b. at New York City, April 7, 1867. Lawyer.

JOSEPH RALPH ENSIGN   *Simsbury, Conn.*
  M.A. b. at Simsbury, Conn., Nov. 24, 1868. m. Manufacturing business.

CHARLES FOSTER KENT   *Providence, R. I.*
  Ph.D. b. at Palmyra, N. Y., Aug. 13, 1867. m. Prof. of
Biblical Literature and History at Brown. Member of
American Oriental Society, and of Die Deutschen Mor-
genländischen Gessellschaft.

WILLIAM ADOLPH McQUAID   *New York City.*
  LL.B. b. at Webster, Mass., Oct. 3, 1865. Lawyer.

WILLIAM HERBERT PAGE   *Salt Lake City, Utah.*
  b. at Mt. Union, O., Aug. 6, 1866. Teacher.

HARRY LATHROP REED   *Auburn, N. Y.*
  b. at Port Byron, N. Y., Dec. 15, 1867. Minister.

OLIVER HUNTINGTON RICHARDSON   *New Haven, Conn.*
  b. at Providence, R. I., Dec. 22, 1866. Ass't Prof. of Hist.
at Yale.

FERDINAND SCHWILL   *Chicago, Ill.*
  Ph.D. Freiburg. b. at Cincinnati, O., Nov. 12, 1868.
Instructor in History at U. of Chicago.

EDMUND DANIEL SCOTT   *New Haven, Conn.*
  Ph.D. b. at New Haven, Conn., Feb. 6, 1866. Teacher.

HERBERT AUGUSTINE SMITH   *New Haven, Conn.*
  b. at Southampton, Mass., Dec. 6, 1866. m. Instructor
in English at Yale.

HORACE FLETCHER WALKER
  b. at Detroit, Mich., July 11, 1868. Instructor in French
at Yale. d 1894.

ANDREW LUDWIG WINTERS   *Chicago, Ill.*
  b. at Reading, Pa., Oct. 11, 1864. m. Lawyer.

GEORGE WASHINGTON WOODRUFF   *Philadelphia, Pa.*
  LL.B. U. of P. b. at Dimock, Pa., Feb. 22, 1864. Lawyer.

HORACE WYLIE   *Washington, D. C.*
  LL.B. Harv. b. at Washington, D. C., Sept. 16, 1869. m.
Lawyer.

1890

GEORGE L. AMERMAN   *Marcellus, N. Y.*
Ph.D. b. at Chicago, Ill., Dec. 14, 1865. Asst. in Chemistry at Yale.

ROGER SHERMAN BALDWIN   *New Haven, Conn.*
LL.B., M.L. b. at New Haven, Conn., Jan. 17, 1869. Lawyer.

FREDERICK BEDELL   *Ithaca, N. Y.*
Ph.D. b. at Brooklyn, N. Y., April 13, 1868. Ass't Professor of Physics at Cornell.

FRANK TERRY BROOKS   *Greenwich, Conn.*
M.D. L. I. Coll. Hosp. b. at Haverhill, Mass., Feb. 15, 1867. Physician.

JOHN CROSBY   *Minneapolis, Minn.*
b. at Hampton, Me., Aug. 23, 1867. Lawyer.

WALTER ALDEN DeCAMP   *Cincinnati, O.*
b. at Madisonville, O., April 27, 1868. Lawyer.

WALTER DENNIS
d. 1889.

HENRY THATCHER FOWLER   *Galesburg, Ill.*
b. at Fishkill, N. Y., March 4, 1867. Professor of Ethics at Knox U.

GEORGE WILLIAM GEDNEY   *New York City.*
b. at Newburgh, N. Y., May 17, 1868. Lawyer.

CHARLES HUMPHREY HAMILL   *Chicago, Ill.*
b. at Chicago, Ill., March 20, 1868. Lawyer.

LEWIS SCOFIELD HASLAM   *New York City.*
LL.B. b. at Stamford, Conn., Aug. 29, 1866. Lawyer.

ELLIOTT PROCTOR JOSLIN   *Boston, Mass.*
Ph.B. b. at Oxford, Mass., June 6, 1869. Physician.

YALE KNEELAND   *New York City.*
b. at Brooklyn, N. Y., Aug. 5, 1869. Grain business.

WILLIAM APPLETON McCONNEL.   *Beaver, Pa.*
b. at West Bridgewater, Pa., Oct. 23, 1866. Lawyer.

FRANK SHERMAN MEARA   *New York City.*
     b. at Salem, Mass., May 6, 1866.   Physician.   Ass't
     in Physiol. Chem. at Yale.

SIDNEY NELSON MORSE   *Easthampton, Mass.*
     b. at North Woodstock, Conn., Nov. 29, 1857.   Teacher.
     in Williston Academy.

HARRY LOOMIS MUNGER   *Dayton, O.*
     b. at Dayton, O., March 16, 1868.   Lawyer.

HENRY OPDYKE   *New York City.*
     b. at Brooklyn, N. Y., Aug. 27, 1870.   Lawyer.

NATHAN TODD PORTER   *New York City.*
     b. at Brooklyn, N. Y., Dec. 5, 1867.   Business.

CHARLES FRANCIS SMALL   *New Haven, Conn.*
     b. at Pawtucket, R. I., July 11, 1869.   Business.

1891

GROSVENOR ATTERBURY   *New York City.*
     b. at Detroit, Mich., July 7, 1869.   Architect.

CECIL KITTREDGE BANCROFT   *New Haven, Conn.*
     b. at Lookout Mountain, Tenn., Dec. 15, 1868.   Tutor in
     Latin at Yale.

WILLIAM TENNEY BARTLEY   *Salem, N. H.*
     Ph.D.   b. at Concord, N. H., Nov. 7, 1868.   Minister.

JOSEPH BOWDEN   *Dobbs Ferry, N. Y.*
     Ph.D.   b. in Cornwall, Eng., Feb. 10, 1869.   Teacher at
     Westminster School.

FRANCIS THEODORE BROWN   *North Adams, Mass.*
     b. at Troy, N. Y., April 26, 1869.   Minister.

CURTIS CLARK BUSHNELL   *New Haven, Conn.*
     Ph.D.   b. at New Haven, Conn., Aug. 10, 1876.   Teacher.

DUANE PHILLIPS COBB   *Orange, N. J.*
     b. at Kankakee, Ill., Nov. 14, 1867.   Lawyer.

JOHN JOUGHIN COX
     b. at Bedford, N. Y., Sept. 28, 1869.   d. 1892.

FRANK CRAWFORD   *Omaha, Neb.*
    LL.B. Michigan. b. at Colebrook, N. H., March 12, 1870.
    Lawyer.

FRANK AYER DILLINGHAM   *Summit, N. J.*
    LL.B. Col. b. at New York City, Dec. 31, 1869. Lawyer.

EDWARD PAYSON DREW   *Stowe, Vt.*
    M.A., B.D. Chicago Theol. Sem. b. at Cabot, Vt., Nov. 1,
    1868. Minister.

JOE GARNER ESTILL   *Lakeville, Conn.*
    M.A. b. at Winchester, Tenn., Oct. 2, 1863. m. Teacher
    in Hotchkiss School.

RAYMOND HILLIARD GAGE   *Wenonah, N. J.*
    M.A. Princeton. b. at Dover, N. J., Aug. 31, 1869. m.
    Minister.

NATHAN GLICKSMAN   *Milwaukee, Wis.*
    b. at Chippewa Falls, Wis., June 14, 1870. Lawyer.

HIPPOLYTE WASHINGTON GRUENER   *Cleveland, O.*
    Ph.D. b. at New Haven, Conn., Feb. 22, 1869. Instructor
    at Western Reserve.

CHARLES PRENTICE HOWLAND   *New York City.*
    M.A., LL.B. Harv.* b. at New York City, Sept. 15, 1869.
    Lawyer. Civil service examiner.

HOWARD THAYER KINGSBURY   *New York City.*
    LL.B. N. Y. L. S. b. at Rome, N. Y., April 1, 1870.
    Lawyer.

EDWARD NATHANIEL LOOMIS   *New York City.*
    b. at Brooklyn, N. Y., June 6, 1869. Lawyer.

LAFAYETTE BENEDICT MENDEL   *New Haven, Conn.*
    Ph.D. b. at Delhi, N. Y., Feb. 5, 1872. Asst. Prof. of
    Physiological Chemistry at Yale.

HARRY LEROY PANGBORN   *New York City.*
    b. at Jersey City, N. J., April 19, 1870. m. Mining busi-
    ness.

SAMUEL CARTER SHAW   *Redding Ridge, Conn.*
    b. at Redding Ridge, Conn., Nov. 3, 1866. Teacher.
    Lawyer.

   7

FRANCIS LOUIS SLADE *New York City.*
b. at New York City, April 11, 1870. Banking business.

HERBERT KNOX SMITH *Hartford, Conn.*
LL.B. b. at Chester, Mass., Nov. 17, 1869. Lawyer.

RAY BURDICK SMITH *Syracuse, N. Y.*
b. at Cuyler, N. Y., Dec. 11, 1867. Lawyer.

WILLIAM NEVIN THATCHER
b. at Pueblo, Col., Dec. 3, 1870. d. 1891.

LUTHER HENRY TUCKER *Albany, N. Y.*
M.A. b. at Albany, N. Y., Sept. 9, 1869. m. Editor.

HENRY HALLAM TWEEDY *Binghamton, N. Y.*
b. at Binghamton, N. Y., Aug., 1868. Minister.

CLIFFORD GRAY TWOMBLY *Newton, Mass.*
B.D. Cambr. Episc. Theol. b. at Stamford, Conn., May 7,
1869. Minister.

1892

BERNARD MELZAR ALLEN *Andover, Mass.*
b. at Walpole, Mass., Dec. 19, 1869. m. Instructor at
Phillips Academy.

CHARLES JOSEPH BARTLETT ✱ *New Haven, Conn.*
M.A., M.D. b. at Sutton, Vt., Dec. 18, 1864. Ass't Prof.
of Pathology in Yale Medical School.

WILLIAM BRADFORD BOSLEY *San Francisco, Cal.*
LL.B. b. at Livonia, N. Y., May 9, 1865. m. Asst.
Prof. in Law Dept. U. of Cal.

FRED CLARK GALLUP BRONSON *Norwich, Conn.*
b. at Wallingford, Conn., Jan. 13, 1871. m.

GEORGE WETMORE COLLES *Hoboken, N. J.*
M.E. Stevens Inst. of Technology. b. at New York City,
Feb. 16, 1871.

CLIVE HART DAY *Berkeley, Cal.*
Ph.D. b. at Hartford, Conn., Feb. 11, 1871. Asst. Prof.
of History in U. of Cal.

PERCY FINLAY *Memphis, Tenn.*
LL.B. b. at Memphis, Tenn., July 15, 1872. Lawyer.

HIRAM FOBES   *Lakeville, Mass.*
    LL.B. N. Y. Law School. b. at Scituate, R. I., Oct. 19,
1865. Lawyer.

GEORGE HERBERT GIRTY   *Washington, D. C.*
    Ph.D. b. at Cleveland, O., Dec. 30, 1869. U. S. Geolog-
ical Survey.

HENRY BARRETT HINCKLEY   *Northampton, Mass.*
    b. at Northampton, Mass., March 1, 1871. Teacher.

WILLIAM JAMES HUTCHINS   *Oberlin, O.*
    b. at Brooklyn, N. Y., July 5, 1871. m. Minister.

JAMES WERNHAM DUNSFORD INGERSOLL   *New Haven, Conn.*
    Ph.D. b. at Marengo, Ill., Sept. 18, 1867. Ass't Prof.
of Latin at Yale.

WILLIAM LLOYD KITCHEL   *New York City.*
    LL.B. b. at New Haven, Conn., Nov. 30, 1869. m.
Lawyer.

JAMES HALL MASON KNOX   *Baltimore, Md.*
    Ph.D., M.A. Lafayette. b. at Philadelphia, Pa., May 20,
1872.

ELLIOTT MARSHALL   *Montclair, N. J.*
    LL.B. N. Y. Law School. b. at Jersey City, N. J., Oct.
11, 1870. m. Lawyer.

ALFRED BARNES PALMER
    d. 1892.

MATTHEW AMBROSE REYNOLDS   *New Haven, Conn.*
    LL.B. b. at North Branford, Conn., March 10, 1871.
Lawyer.

ISAAC WOODBRIDGE RILEY   *New Haven, Conn.*
    b. at New York City, May 20, 1869. Minister.

CHARLES AUGUSTUS SCHUMAKER   *Parish, N. Y.*
    Ph.D. b. at Clay, N. Y., Dec. 28, 1868. Teacher.

CHARLES BROWN SEARS   *Buffalo, N. Y.*
    LL.B. b. at Brooklyn, N. Y., Oct. 16, 1870. Lawyer.

FRANK WRIGHT SEYMOUR   *Winsted, Conn.*
    LL.B. b. at Colebrook, Conn., Aug. 7, 1871. Lawyer.

ARTHUR WYNNE SHAW   *New York City.*
   M.A. b. at Wilmington, Del., Nov. 3, 1870. Teacher.

JAMES EVERETT WHEELER   *New Haven, Conn.*
   LL.B. b. at New Haven, Conn., Dec. 24, 1870. Lawyer.

ALBERT LAVINE WHITTAKER   *Clinton, Mo.*
   b. at Wallingford, Conn., May 5, 1871. Teacher. Minister.

1893

WILLIAM REYNOLDS BEGG   *St. Paul, Minn.*
   b. at Spartanburg, S. C., Feb. 12, 1869. m. Lawyer.

CHARLES WILDER BOSWORTH   *Springfield, Mass.*
   b. at Springfield, Mass., Aug. 28, 1871. Lawyer.

HOWARD SIDNEY BOWNS   *New York City.*
   b. at Brooklyn, N. Y., Jan. 28, 1873. Business.

THOMAS IVES CHATFIELD   *New York City.*
   LL.B. Col. b. at Owego, N. Y., Oct. 4, 1871. Lawyer.

GEORGE MASON CREEVEY   *New York City.*
   M.D. P. and S. b. at Town of Hope, N. Y., July 4, 1872.
   Surgeon.

WINTHROP EDWARDS DWIGHT   *New Haven, Conn.*
   LL.B., Ph.D. b. at New Haven, Conn., Sept. 23, 1872.

CHARLES BROWN EDDY   *New York City.*
   LL.B. N. Y. Law School. b. at New Britain, Conn., Nov.
   29, 1872. Lawyer.

CHARLES HULL EWING   *Chicago, Ill.*
   b. at Randolph, N. Y., July 11, 1868.

CHARLES JARVIS FAY   *Hartford, Conn.*
   b. at Columbus, O., Aug. 26, 1871.

JAMES EDWARD GRAFTON   *Waterbury, Conn.*
   b. at Norwich, Conn., July 27, 1871. Teacher.

FRANK WILLIAM HASTINGS   *Bradford, Pa.*
   b. at Franklin, Pa., Dec. 8, 1869. Lawyer.

LOGAN HAY   *Springfield, Ill.*
   LL.B. Harv. b. at Springfield, Ill., Feb. 13, 1871. Lawyer.

THEODORE WOOLSEY HEERMANCE   *New Haven, Conn.*
b. at New Haven, Conn., March 22, 1872.   Tutor at Yale.

WILLIAM JUDSON LAMSON   *Boston, Mass.*
b. at Orange, N. J., May 14, 1871.   Publisher.

IRVING PHILLIPS LYON   *Baltimore, Md.*
M.D. Johns Hopkins.   b. at Hartford, Conn., Jan. 12,
1870.   Pathologist.

ALFRED KINDRED MERRITT   *New Haven, Conn.*
b. at Weldon, N. J., Nov. 26, 1866.   Registrar of Yale College.

ALTON WILLIAM PEIRCE   *New Haven, Conn.*
b. at New Salem, Mass., Sept. 25, 1868.   Instructor in
Chemistry at Yale.

GEORGE HOWARD RICE   *Phoenix, Arizona.*
b. at Springfield, Mass., Sept. 22, 1866.   Lawyer.

LOUIS BARCROFT RUNK   *Philadelphia, Pa.*
LL.B. U. of P.   b. at Philadelphia, June 13, 1872.   Lawyer.

WENDELL MELVILLE STRONG   *New Haven, Conn.*
b. at Indianapolis, Ind., Feb. 6, 1871.   Instructor in Mathematics at Yale.

HARRY SELDEN VAILE   *Oak Park, Ill.*
b. at Columbus, O., April 22, 1871.   Teacher.

ISIDORE WACHSMAN   *Albany, N. Y.*
LL.B. Albany.   b. at Brooklyn, N. Y., July 11, 1870.
Lawyer.

JOHN DORRANCE WARNOCK   *Geneva, N. Y.*
b. at Geneva, N. Y., Feb. 11, 1868.

LEMUEL AIKEN WELLES   *New York City.*
LL.B. N. Y. Law School.   b. at Newington, Conn., Nov.
18, 1870.   Lawyer.

ARTHUR LESLIE WHEELER   *New Haven, Conn.*
b. at Hartford, Conn., Aug. 12, 1871.   m.   Instructor in
Latin at Yale.

ALBERT BEEBE WHITE   *New Haven, Conn.*
b. at Holbrook, Mass., Sept. 11, 1871.   m.

ALFRED CHARLES WOOLNER   *New York City.*
LL.B.   b. at Louisville, Ky., March 14, 1872.   Lawyer.

1894

SAMUEL STOKES ALLEN   *Philadelphia, Pa.*
   b. at Philadelphia, Pa., Feb. 8, 1874.

GUSTAV ALBERT ANDREEN   *New Haven, Conn.*
   b. at Baileytown, Ind., March 13, 1864.   Tutor in German
   at Yale.

EDWARD RICHMOND BOSLEY   *Buffalo, N. Y.*
   b. at Geneseo, N. Y., Aug. 9, 1869.

HENRY WALTER BUNN   *Andover, Mass.*
   b. at Morris, N. Y., May 29, 1875.   Teacher.

FRANK HERBERT CHASE
   b. at Portland, Me., April 22, 1870.   Teacher.

JOSEPH PLATT COOKE   *Oakland, Cal.*
   b. at Honolulu, H. I., Dec. 15, 1870.   Business.

THOMAS FREDERICK DAVIES   *New York City.*
   b. at Philadelphia, Pa., July 20, 1872.   Minister.

HENRY SHEPHERD DAWSON   *New Haven, Conn.*
   b. at New Haven, Conn., June 22, 1872.

ARTHUR GILLESPIE DICKSON   *Philadelphia, Pa.*
   b. at Philadelphia, Pa., Nov. 17, 1873.

GEORGE ELIAS DORLAND   *Buffalo, N. Y.*
   b. at Orchard Park, N. Y., Aug. 13, 1869.

ARTHUR WELLS ELTING   *Baltimore, Md.*
   b. at So. Cairo, N. Y., Oct. 6, 1872.

WINFRED ERNEST GARRISON   *St. Louis, Mo.*
   b. at St. Louis, Mo., Oct. 1, 1874.   Journalist.

LOUIS PACKARD GILLESPIE   *New York City.*
   b. at Brooklyn, N. Y., Jan. 2, 1872.   Business.

THOMAS WARRINGTON GOSLING   *Cincinnati, O.*
   b. at Mt. Airy, O., Sept. 15, 1872.   Teacher.

HERBERT HUMPHREY KELLOGG   *Brooklyn, N. Y.*
   b. at Warsaw, N. Y., Sept. 14, 1872.   Lawyer.

ERNEST KNAEBEL   *New Haven, Conn.*
   b. at Roslyn, L. I., June 14, 1872.   Lawyer.

ROBERT HASTINGS NICHOLS   *Pottstown, Pa.*
  b. at Rochester, N. Y., Oct. 2, 1873. Teacher.

HENRY SHORE NOON   *Cambridge, Mass.*
  b. at Needham, Mass., April 10, 1873.

CHARLES GROSVENOR OSGOOD   *New Haven, Conn.*
  b. at Wellsborough, Pa., May 4, 1871. Graduate student
  in English at Yale.

WILLIAM MINER RAYMOND   *Chicago, Ill.*
  b. at Evanston, Ill., Nov. 23, 1872.

EDWARD BLISS REED   *New Haven, Conn.*
  Ph.D. b. at Lansingburg, N. Y., Aug. 19, 1872. Tutor
  in English at Yale.   .

PHILIP FLETCHER ROGERS   *Chicago, Ill.*
  b. at Milwaukee, Wis., Aug. 14, 1870.

CHARLES RIVES SKINKER   *St. Louis, Mo.*
  b. at St. Louis, Mo., Dec. 18, 1870. Lawyer.

REST FENNER SMITH
  b. at Brooklyn, N. Y., May 8, 1870.

EDWARD RUSSELL THOMAS   *New York City.*
  b. at Columbus, O., Dec. 30, 1873.

WILLIAM EDWARD THOMS   *Waterbury, Conn.*
  b. at Plymouth, Conn., Dec. 22, 1870. Lawyer.

WILLARD GIBBS VANNAME   *New Haven, Conn.*
  b. at New Haven, Conn., April 18, 1872.

GEORGE FINCK VANSLYCK
  b. at Montclair, N. J., Jan. 24, 1874.

SHELTON KING WHEELER   *Chattanooga, Tenn.*
  b. at Chattanooga, Tenn., Aug. 13, 1872.

HARRY PAYNE WHITNEY   *New York City.*
  b. at New York City, April 29, 1872. m.

WILLIAM RUNK WRIGHT   *New York City.*
  b. at New York City, Aug. 29, 1873. Business.

1895

HENRY ANDREW BAKER   *Union Hill, N. Y.*
b. at Webster, N. Y., Aug. 3, 1867.

WILLOUGHBY PIERCE BEAM   *Buffalo, N. Y.*
b. at Buffalo, N. Y., Oct. 27, 1871.

SAMUEL FAYERWEATHER BEARDSLEY   *Bridgeport, Conn.*
b. at Bridgeport, Conn., April 7, 1874.

JULIAN CONE BINGHAM   *Northampton, Mass.*
b. at Willimantic, June 5, 1873.

CLEMENT GEORGE CLARKE   *New Haven, Conn.*
b. at Honey Pot, N. Y., Feb. 21, 1869. Tutor in Mathematics at Yale.

FREDERICK MARCY DEFOREST   *Bridgeport, Conn.*
b. at Bridgeport, Conn., Aug. 10, 1872.

JOHN JOSEPH DUNN   *New Haven, Conn.*
b. at New Haven, Conn., Aug. 1871.

ARTHUR HIBBERT EGGLESTON   *New London, Conn.*
b. at New London, Conn., May 30, 1872.

JOHN ELLIOTT   *New Haven, Conn.*
b. at Cranford, N. J., June 8, 1865.

ELMORE FRANKLIN ELMORE   *Troy, N. Y.*
b. at Troy, N. Y., July 31, 1873.

PHILIP SAFFERY EVANS   *New Haven, Conn.*
b. at Willimantic, Conn., Aug. 18, 1870.

SAMUEL ALEXANDER EVERITT   *Scarsdale, N. Y.*
b. at Branchville, N. J., March 5, 1871.

EDWARD RIDLEY FINCH   *Plainfield, N. J.*
b. at New York City, Nov. 15, 1873.

GEORGE JAY GIBSON   *Peoria, Ill.*
b. at Cleveland, O., March 17, 1873.

FRANCIS BURTON HARRISON   *New York City.*
b. at New York City, Dec. 18, 1873.

SHIRLEY TREADWAY HIGH   *Chicago, Ill.*
b. at Chicago, Ill., March 20, 1874.

LOUIS HALSEY HOLDEN   *Newark, N. J.*
   b. at Newark, N. J.. Aug. 7, 1873.

GEORGE JACOBUS   *Springfield, Mass.*
   b. at New Brighton, Pa., May 12, 1872.

EDWARD CLINTON JONES   *New Haven, Conn.*
   b. at New Haven, Conn., May 5, 1870.

GEORGE DWIGHT KELLOGG   *New Haven, Conn.*
   b. at St. Louis, Mo., June 28, 1873.   Proctor at Yale.

EDWARD GRIDLEY KENDALL   *New Haven, Conn.*
   b. at So. Amenia, N. Y., May 31, 1877.

NORTON ADAMS KENT   *Fordham Heights, N. Y.*
   b. at New York City, July 28, 1873.

CHARLES ADAMS KIMBALL   *Littleton, Mass.*
   b. at Littleton, Mass., Feb. 23, 1867.

GEORGE AUGUSTUS LEWIS   *Hudson, N. Y.*
   b. at Bedford, N. Y., Nov. 13, 1874.

EDWIN CARLYLE LOBENSTINE   *New York City.*
   b. at Leavenworth, Kan. Jan. 18, 1872.

EUGENE ISAAC MEYER   *New York City.*
   b. at Los Angeles, Cal., Oct. 31, 1875.

HERBERT CHESTER NUTTING   *Mt. Vernon, N. Y.*
   b. at New York City, Jan. 14, 1872.

WILLIAM EDWARD PARSONS   *Akron, O.*
   b. at New York City, March 7, 1872.

TRACY PECK   *New York City.*
   b. at Ithaca, N. Y., April 1, 1874.   Business.

WILLIAM MARTIN RICHARDS   *New York City.*
   b. at New Haven, Conn., March 31, 1873.   Physician.

ARTHUR BEHN SHEPLEY   *St. Louis, Mo.*
   b. at St. Louis, Mo.. March 25, 1873.

ALBURN EDWARD SKINNER   *Westfield, N. Y.*
   b. at Westfield, N. Y., Feb. 3, 1873.

HARRY LOCKMAN STREET   *Chicago, Ill.*
   b. at Chicago, Ill., Feb. 26, 1871.

GEORGE STEDMAN SUMNER   *Claremont, Cal.*
    b. at Monson, Mass., Oct. 24, 1874.

CHARLES STOREY THURSTON   *Whitinsville, Mass.*
    b. at Whitinsville, Mass., April 17, 1872.

SAMUEL TYLER   *Boston, Mass.*
    b. at Minneapolis, Minn., March 11, 1871.

CHARLES HEALD WELLER   *Watkins, N. Y.*
    b. at Tyrone, N. Y., Nov. 7, 1870.

ROGER WIDDINGTON WHINFIELD   *Fond du Lac, Wis.*
    b. at Beaver Dam, Wis., March 9, 1874.

1896

JOHN SEXTON ABERCROMBIE   *Rushville, Ind.*
    b. at Rushville, Ind., May 12, 1874.

JOHN CHESTER ADAMS   *Brookline, Mass.*
    b. at Lewiston, Me., Sept. 20, 1873.

EUGENE DAVENPORT ALEXANDER   *New Brighton, N. Y.*
    b. at New Brighton, N. Y., May 10, 1875.

PHILIP RAY ALLEN   *Walpole, Mass.*
    b. at Allenville, Mass., July 25, 1873.

SAMUEL MORGAN ALVORD   *Bolton, Conn.*
    b. at Bolton, Conn., Nov. 19, 1869.

WILLIAM GIDEON BAKER   *Buckeystown, Md.*
    b. at Buckeystown, Md., Dec. 21, 1874.

FRED FOX BENNETT   *Hartford, Conn.*
    b. at Hartford, Conn., Feb. 24, 1870.

ALEXANDER GAENER BENTLEY   *Washington, D. C.*
    b. at Washington, D. C., Oct. 6, 1875.

JOHN MILTON BERDAN   *New York City.*
    b. at Toledo, O., July 9, 1873.

ARTHUR WALKER BINGHAM   *West Cornwall, Vt.*
    b. at West Cornwall, Vt., April 13, 1873.

CHARLES WILLIAM BIRELY   *Frederick, Md.*
    b. at Frederick, Md., Dec. 13, 1874.

HARVEY WOOD CHAPMAN   *Bridgeport, Conn.*
  b. at Stratford, Conn., Feb. 22, 1875.

EDWARD CONNOR CHICKERING   *Exeter, N. H.*
  b. at Exeter, N. H., Feb. 19, 1875.

WALTER HAVEN CLARK   *Hartford, Conn.*
  b. at Hartford, Conn., Jan. 20, 1872.

CHRISTOPHER BUSH COLEMAN   *Springfield, Ill.*
  b. at Springfield, Ill., April 24, 1875.

CHARLES COLLINS   *New Haven, Conn.*
  b, at New York City, Oct. 14, 1873.

EDWARD DAY COLLINS   *Barton Landing, Vt.*
  b. at Hardwick, Vt., Dec. 17, 1869.   Asst. in History at
  Yale.

LEWIS ROBERTS CONKLIN   *Monroe, N. Y.*
  b. at Monroe, N. Y., Oct. 10, 1874.

SHERMAN DAY   *New York City.*
  b. at New York City, Sept. 7, 1874.

EDWARD EVERETT DENISON   *Marion, Ill.*
  b. at Marion, Ill., Aug. 28, 1873.

SHERWOOD OWEN DICKERMAN   *New Haven, Conn.*
  b. at Lewiston, Me., Nov. 23, 1874.

FRANK PHELPS DODGE

EDWARD LEWIS DURFEE   *Palmyra, N. Y.*
  b. at Palmyra, N. Y., Jan. 26, 1875.

JAY GLOVER ELDRIDGE   *Penfield, N. Y.*
  b. at Janesville, Wis., Nov. 8, 1875.

HOLLON AUGUSTINE FARR   *Athol, Mass.*
  b. at Athol, Mass., Sept. 2, 1872.

JOHN MARSHALL GAINES   *New Haven, Conn.*
  b. at New Haven, Conn., May 11, 1873.   Asst. in Pol.
  Econ. at Yale.

WILLIAM STANDISH GAYLORD   *Norwich, Conn.*
  b. at Meriden, Conn., March 14, 1874.

THEODORE MEECH GOWANS   *Buffalo, N. Y.*
  b. at Buffalo, N. Y., July 19, 1874.

HERBERT ERNEST GREGORY   *New Haven, Conn.*
b. at Middleville, Mich., Oct. 15, 1869.

MAITLAND GRIGGS   *Hartford, Conn.*
b. at Granby, Conn., Feb. 12, 1872.

HERBERT EDWIN HAWKES   *Templeton, Mass.*
b. at Templeton, Mass., Dec. 6, 1872. m. Instructor in
Math. at Yale.

WILLIAM LESTER HENRY   *Plattsburg, N. Y.*
b. at Plattsburg, N. Y., June 26, 1874.

WILLIAM MILTON HESS   *New Haven, Conn.*
b. at Philadelphia, Pa., June 26, 1870.

ALBERT GALLOWAY KELLER   *Milford, Conn.*
b. at Springfield, O., April 10, 1874.

FREDERICK STEPHEN JACKSON   *Waterbury, Conn.*
b. at Waterbury, Conn., July 10, 1873.

FRANK MASON JEFFREY   *Torrington, Conn.*
b. at Torrington, Conn., Aug. 9, 1874.

LOUIS CLEVELAND JONES   *East Durham, N. Y.*
b. at Oak Hill, N. Y., Dec. 24, 1871.

ROBERT STEWART McCLENAHAN   *Tarkio, Mo.*
b. at Wyoming, Iowa, June 5, 1871.

HENRY EDWIN McDERMOTT   *New Haven, Conn.*
b. at St. John, N. B., Nov. 27, 1873.

McKEE DUNN McKEE   *Washington, D. C.*
b. at Washington, D. C., Oct. 21, 1873.

WILLIAM CONGER MORGAN   *Albany, N. Y.*
b. at Albany, N. Y., June 21, 1874.

GEORGE HENRY NETTLETON   *New Haven, Conn.*
b. at Boston, Mass., July 16, 1874.

HENRY AUGUSTUS PERKINS   *Hartford, Conn.*
b. at Hartford, Conn., Nov. 14, 1873.

LOUIS HOPKINS PORTER   *Stamford, Conn.*
b. at New York City, March 16, 1874.

ADDISON STRONG PRATT   *Fairport, N. Y.*
b. at Chaumont, N. Y., May 4, 1873.

WALTER FRANKLIN PRINCE   *Detroit, Me.*
  b. at Detroit, Me., April 22, 1863.

FRED OSCAR ROBBINS   *New York City.*
  b. at Greenville, N. H., Feb. 12, 1870.

EDWIN LOOMIS ROBINSON   *Lebanon, Conn.*
  b. at Lebanon, Conn., March 2, 1870.

SYLVESTER BAKER SADLER   *Carlisle, Pa.*
  b. at Carlisle, Pa., Sept. 29, 1876.

LEE RUTLAND SCARBOROUGH   *Waco, Texas.*
  b. at Colfax, La., July 4, 1870.

RUDOLPH SCHWILL   *Cincinnati, O.*
  b. at Cincinnati, O., June 18, 1874.

HEWLETT SCUDDER   *New York City.*
  b. at Northport, L. I., Aug. 9, 1875.

ANSON PHELPS STOKES   *New York City.*
  b. at New Brighton, N. Y., April 13, 1874.

ASA CURRIER TILTON   *Raymond, N. H.*
  b. at Raymond, N. H., April 25, 1872.

ALBERT EUGENE VON TOBEL   *Torrington, Conn.*
  b. at Harwinton, Conn., Aug. 8, 1875.

HOWLAND TWOMBLY   *Newton, Mass.*
  b. at Boston, Mass., April 13, 1875.

WILLIAM HENRY WADHAMS   *New York City.*
  b. at Annapolis, Md., Dec. 7, 1873.

FREDERICK EDWARD WEYERHAEUSER   *Rock Island, Ill.*
  b. at Rock Island, Ill., Nov. 4, 1872.

ROBERT EDWIN WHALEN   *Albany, N. Y.*
  b. at Ballston Spa, N. Y., July 29, 1874.

1897

HERBERT BASSETT AUGER   *Hartford, Conn.*
  b. at Hartford, Conn., June 24, 1874.

EVERETT LARKIN BARNARD   *New York City.*
  b. at Calais, Me., Oct. 14, 1875.

WILLIAM DE VERNE BEACH *New Haven, Conn.*
b. at Bridgeport, Conn.. Dec. 11, 1873.

ARTHUR HARRY BISSELL *Montclair, N. J.*
b. at Washington, D. C., July 9, 1877.

SHELTON BISSELL *Montclair, N. J.*
b. at Washington, D. C., Sept. 4, 1875.

ALFRED GUITNER BOOKWALTER *New Haven, Conn.*
b. in Iowa, Oct. 16, 1873.

GEORGE CLYMER BROOKE *Birdsboro, Pa.*
b. at Birdsboro, Pa., June 5, 1875.

ABRAHAM ROYER BRUBACHER *Shæfferstown, Pa.*
b. at Shæfferstown, Pa., July 27, 1870.

CHARLES MEIGS CHARNLEY *Chicago, Ill.*
b. at Chicago, Ill., May 16, 1874.

WILLARD CHURCH *New York City.*
b. at New York City, March 6, 1875.

WILLIAM CHURCHILL *New Britain, Conn.*
b. at New Britain, Conn., Nov. 3, 1876.

CHARLES UPSON CLARK *Brooklyn, N. Y.*
b. at Springfield, Mass., Jan. 14, 1875.

WILLIAM FRANCIS CLARK *Meriden, Conn.*
b. at Thompsonville, Conn., May 26, 1871.

FRANK MCMILLAN COBB *Cleveland, O.*
b. at Cleveland, O., June 21, 1874.

HENRY SLOANE COFFIN *New York City.*
b. at New York City, Jan. 5, 1877.

WILLIAM HENRY COMLEY *Bridgeport, Conn.*
b. at Bridgeport, Conn., Oct. 12, 1875.

THEODORE MATHEW CONNOR *Northampton, Mass.*
b. at Florence, Mass., April 6, 1875.

FREDERICK BALDWIN CURTIS *Bridgeport, Conn.*
b. at Bridgeport, Conn., June 8, 1875.

GEORGE BARTON CUTTEN *Montowese, Conn.*
b. at Amherst, N. S., April 11, 1874.

WILLIAM DARRACH   *Germantown, Pa.*
  b. at Germantown, Pa., March 12, 1876.

BENJAMIN FRANKLIN EBY   *Chicago, Ill.*
  b. at Sun Hill, Pa., Jan. 27, 1878.

ARTHUR WOOLSEY EWELL   *Washington, D. C.*
  b. at Bradford, Mass., Oct. 20, 1873.

AUGUSTINE WILLIAM FERRIN   *Salamanca, N. Y.*
  b. at Little Valley, N. Y., April 1, 1875.

EMERSON DAVID FITE   *Marion, O.*
  b. at Marion, O., March 3, 1874.

WILLIAM HENRY HARRISON HEWITT   *New Haven, Conn.*
  b. at New Haven, Conn., Feb. 15, 1877.

ALLEN HALL HITCHCOCK   *Meriden, Conn.*
  b. at Pilot Point, Texas, Aug. 15, 1873.

MURRAY SHIPLEY HOWLAND   *Wilmington, Del.*
  b. at Wilmington, Del., Nov. 22, 1874.

EDWARD HICKS HUME   *New Haven, Conn.*
  b. at Ahmednuggar, India, May 13, 1876.

WENDELL PRIME KEELER   *Washingtonville, N. Y.*
  b. at Washingtonville, N. Y., Feb. 17, 1874.

ALBERT EMMETT KENT   *New York City.*
  b. at New York City, Jan. 20, 1876.

CORNELIUS PORTER KITCHELL   *Liverpool, O.*
  b. at East Liverpool, O., Oct. 7, 1875.

JAMES HOYT LEWIS   *Wappingers Falls, N. Y.*
  b. at New Haven, Conn., Aug. 25, 1875.

FREDERICK BLISS LUQUIENS   *New Haven, Conn.*
  b. at Auburndale, Mass., Dec. 10, 1875.

JOHN ROBERT McNEILLE   *New Haven, Conn.*
  b. at Brockton, Mass., Jan. 21, 1876.

WALTER DUNHAM MAKEPEACE   *Springfield, Mass.*
  b. at Gloucester, Mass., April 27, 1875.

ROBERT HUME MILLER   *New Haven, Conn.*
  b. at New Haven, Conn., June 25, 1875.

Blachley Hoyt Porter
b. at Stamford, Conn., Feb. 27, 1876. d. 1895.

John Rush Powell   *Waco, Texas.*
b. at Columbus, Miss., March 21, 1873.

Foster Pruyn   *Albany, N. Y.*
b. at Newark, N. J., Oct. 5, 1875.

Clarence Marsh Reed   *Stamford, Conn.*
b. at Stamford, Conn., May 30, 1876.

Philip Franklin Ripley   *Andover, Mass.*
b. at Andover, Mass., Jan. 19, 1876.

Wallis Gibson Rowe   *Afton, N. Y.*
b. in New York State, April 1, 1867.

Albert Silverstein   *Denver, Col.*
b. at Syracuse, N. Y., April 18, 1875.

Edward Lawrence Smith   *Hartford, Conn.*
b. at Hartford, Conn., Jan. 22, 1875.

Nathan Ayer Smyth   *New Haven, Conn.*
b. at Quincy, Ill., May 29, 1876.

Charles Heitler Studinski   *Pueblo, Col.*
b. at Mansfield, O., April 25, 1876.

Alexander Wheeler   *Bridgeport, Conn.*
b. at Bridgeport, Conn., Nov. 30, 1876.

1898

George Haven Abbott
b. at Charleston, S. C., Oct. 7, 1876.

Robert Woodrow Archbald
b. at Scranton, Pa., Jan. 10, 1876.

Carleton Henry Barclay
b. at Galesburg, Pa., June 17, 1875.

Ashbel Hinman Barney
b. at Irvington on Hudson, July 29, 1876.

Samuel Eliot Bassett
b. at Wilton, Conn., Aug. 11, 1873.

NORMAN BUCKINGHAM BEECHER
    b. at Hillsboro, O., July 22, 1877.

ENOCH FRY BELL
    b. at North Hadley, Mass., May 26, 1874.

FRANKLIN HENDRICKSON BOOTH
    b. at Newtown, N. Y., Nov. 19, 1876.

GEORGE ALEXANDER BRIDGE
    b. at Hazardville, Conn., Jan. 25, 1873.

ZENAS MARSTON BRIGGS
    b. at New Bedford, Mass., April 14, 1876.

NOAH ARTHUR BURR
    b. at Goshen, Conn., March 28, 1875.

AUGUSTUS WILSON CLAPP
    b. at Hudson, Wis., Feb. 9, 1877.

RUSSELL ERVIN COLCORD
    b. at Peabody, Mass., Sept. 18, 1876.

MOLTON AVERY COLTON
    b. at Indian Territory, 1872.

EDGAR SELAH DOWNS
    b. at Southington, Conn., Sept. 25, 1874.

WILLIAM GAGE ERVING
    b. at Hartford, Conn., Aug. 11, 1877.

CHARLES EVERETT FARR
    b. at Athol, Mass., Oct. 10, 1875.

MORTON LAZELL FEAREY
    b. at Albany, N. Y., Nov. 17, 1876.

HERBERT WESTCOTT FISHER
    b. at Peacedale, R. I., Dec. 14, 1873.

HENRY FLETCHER
    b. at Brooklyn, N. Y., Sept. 29, 1877.

WILLIAM RUTHVEN FLINT
    b. at McIndoes Falls, Vt., April 12, 1875.

CHARLES BROWNELL GAGE
    b. at Astoria, L. I., April 14, 1874.

8

MORRELL WALKER GAINES
b. at Litchfield, Conn., Jan. 28, 1875.

ARTHUR THOMAS GALT
b. at Chicago, Ill., Sept. 8, 1876.

RICHARD BUTLER GLAENZER
b. at Paris, France, Dec. 15, 1876.

PHILIP SANFORD GOULDING
b. at Rutland, Vt., Sept. 6, 1876.

CHARLES WELLES GROSS
b. at Hartford, Conn., Oct. 13, 1876.

HAROLD AMES HATCH
b. at Brooklyn, Conn., Sept. 30, 1876.

ABNER PIERCE HAYES
b. at Bethlehem, Conn., Jan. 25, 1876.

CHARLES POTTER HINE
b. at Poland, O., Sept. 5, 1877.

PETER HAGNER HOLME
b. at Denver, Col., Feb. 12, 1877.

ROBERT ERNEST HUME
b. at Ahmednagar, India, March 22, 1877.

LEEDS JOHNSON
b. at New Brighton, N. Y., April 16, 1875.

FREDERICK AUGUST LEHLBACH
b. at Newark, N. J., Feb. 2, 1875.

LOUIS SAMTER LEVY
b. at Forkland, Ala., Aug. 7, 1877.

SYDNEY KNOX MITCHELL
b. at Lakeville, N. Y., Jan. 28, 1875.

ERNEST CLAP NOYES
b. at Woodbury, Conn., May 5, 1877.

WILLIAM HAZEN PECK
b. at New Britain, Conn., Oct. 5, 1875.

EDWARD CARTER PERKINS
b. at Hartford, Conn., July 11, 1875.

LEMUEL GARDNER PETTEE
b. at Sharon, Mass., April 10, 1875.

ROBERT KIMBALL RICHARDSON
b. at Hartford, Conn., June 6, 1876.

GEORGE MINOT RIPLEY
b. at St. Louis, Mo., Jan. 3, 1876.

ROBERT KILBURN ROOT
b. at Brooklyn, N. Y., April 7, 1877.

FRANK HIRAM SHALL
b. at Little Falls, N. Y., 1875.

HENRY SILLCOCKS
b. at Brooklyn, N. Y., July 10, 1876.

JAMES ROBINSON SMITH
b. at Hartford, Conn., Dec. 27, 1876.

FRANK RAYMOND STOCKER
b. at Jermyn, Pa., July 24, 1876.

CHARLES HOWARD TEETER
b. at East Stroudsburg, Conn., Aug. 1, 1873.

ALFRED HOWE TERRY
b. at Knoxville, Tenn., Nov. 29, 1875.

WILMOT HAINES THOMPSON
b. at Fairfield, N. J., April 5, 1876.

WALTER LEWIS VAUGHAN
b. at Louisville, Ky., June 19, 1875.

CHARLES MCLEAN WARREN
b. at Columbia, S. C., Jan. 12, 1876.

JOHN MUNRO WOOLSEY
b. at Aiken, S. C., Jan. 3, 1877.

HOWARD BROWN WOOLSTON
b. at Harrisburg, Pa., April 22, 1876.

HENRY BURT WRIGHT
b. at New Haven, Conn., Jan. 29, 1877.

MEMBERS-ELECT

1899

SULLIVAN DORR AMES
ROBBINS BATTELL ANDERSON
GEORGE EDWIN ATWOOD
JOHN BOYCE
HENRY THORNTON BOWLES
NORMAN MACLEOD BURRELL
GUY MORTIMER CARLETON
JOHN DOLPH CARSON
JOHN KIRKLAND CLARK
WILLIAM DICK CUTTER
JOHN LEWIS EVANS
WILLARD ERNEST EVERETT
CALEB ELLIS FISHER
JOHN FRANCIS FLYNN
CHARLES ROOT FOWLER
LUCIUS POMEROY FULLER
STEWART GILMAN
ALFRED BATES HALL
FRANCIS JENKS HALL
CHARLES MONTGOMERY HATHAWAY
ARTHUR WAYLAND LOVELL
ARTHUR SITGREAVES MANN
BALLINGER MILLS
JOSEPH HARRISON MOREY
FREDERICK HITCHCOCK MORLEY
WILLIAM BIGELOW NEERGAARD
HENRY JAMES NICHOLS
HIBBARD RICHARD NORMAN
JOHN PEASE NORTON
HOWARD CHANDLER ROBBINS
HENRY ROBINSON SHIPMAN
BARRY CONGAR SMITH
CARL BOVEE SPITZER
CHAUNCEY BREWSTER TINKER
RALPH GIBBS VANNAME

INDEX

Lightning Source UK Ltd.
Milton Keynes UK
UKHW021041110119
335297UK00012B/1678/P